A MOUTH-WATERING SAMPLING FROM "OUR TUSCAN KITCHEN"

*Minestra di lenti
*Beurre Fondu sauce
*Brussels sprouts Milanese style
*Vegetable, herb, and cream soup
*_Pesto_ sauce
*Ravioli alla Fiorentina
*Ribbon noodles with tomatoes,
garlic, and sausages
*Risotto alla Milanese
*Peppers Spanish style
*Tomatoes grilled with mustard dressing
and many more . : .

Mange!

LEAVES FROM OUR TUSCAN KITCHEN

Vegetables as the Center of a Meal

Janet Ross
and
Michael Waterfield

BALLANTINE BOOKS • NEW YORK

Originally published by Atheneum Publishers in 1974.

Library of Congress Catalog Card Number: 74-20667

ISBN 0-345-34621-1

Manufactured in the United States of America

First Ballantine Books Edition: October 1987

Contents

Line drawings in text by Michael Waterfield

Introductory Note

The first edition of this book was published in 1899 by J. M. Dent, and its last, the eleventh, in 1936. Nearly forty years have intervened and copies have become rare, but when found are among the treasured possessions in gourmets' households. There is today a growing interest in good cooking, a change from the end of last century when Janet Ross wrote in her Preface:

> Not so very long ago soup was an exception in English houses—almost a luxury. A dish of vegetables—as a dish and not an adjunct to meat—was a still greater rarity; and even now plain-boiled potatoes, peas, cabbages, etc., are the rule....
>
> For years English friends have begged recipes for cooking vegetables in the Italian fashion, so I have written down many of the following from the dictation of our good Giuseppe Volpi, whose portrait by Mr. A. H. Hallam Murray, adorns this little book, and who has been known to our friends for over thirty years....

Giuseppe was undoubtedly a very fine cook, as were his successors Agostino Sabattini and Carlo Guerrini, for many years a well-known chef in a London City bank. Maria Chiodetti, who still cooks for the family at the Castello della Brunella at Aulla, and worked for some time in the kitchen at Poggio Gherardo there acquiring the tradition of good cooking. Her vegetable dishes are specially appreciated by visitors who stay at the Castle. Janet Ross took great trouble in setting down the recipes from her chefs, to which she added others later. I found, however, that in editing the recipes and using most of them in my restaurant, there were some weights and measured which had to be corrected.

In editing these recipes I have omitted some elaborate dishes. Truffles in champagne, for example, which seems to have been dear to the Edwardians and delicacies which were remote in their aspic are now also remote in their appeal; but the form of the original book remains basically unchanged.

The vegetables are placed alphabetically for immediate reference, with mixed vegetables, salads, rice and spaghetti dishes taking their place at the end. Cross reference should not be necessary as each recipe is complete with its own sauce or manner of serving. All the recipes are for six people.

The lay-out of the recipes has been altered from Janet Ross's narrative form to one where ingredients and method are combined side by side, which should be easier to follow. Oven temperatures and a metric conversion table appear before the recipes.

I had always been interested in my great-great-aunt Janet, having heard about her adventurous life from my family, but it was not until I met the late Sir Harry Luke, who was himself a gourmet and the author of a fine cookery book, that I realised how well-known her book had become in its time. When it was decided to publish a new edition he was kind enough to say that he would like to write about the book and Janet Ross as a Foreword and, to my great pleasure, that is what he did.

The Wife of Bath,
Wye, Kent

MICHAEL WATERFIELD

Foreword

Leaves from our Tuscan Kitchen is the first cookery book I ever possessed; I made its acquaintance on one of the Tuscan holidays of my teenage youth at the same time as I made that of the authoress herself. In the sixty-six years that have elapsed since then I must have earned the gratitude of scores of my women friends through introducing them by means of this precious little volume—a blessing to him that gives no less than to her that takes—to the delights of the best Italian home cooking.

When Janet Ross's *Leaves* made their appearance in the antepenultimate year of Queen Victoria, Mrs. Beeton's monumental work of over a thousand pages still deservedly dominated the English kitchen, perhaps admitting from 1920 onwards in the houses of the more discerning eaters and drinkers the juxtaposition of Professor George Saintsbury's slender classic, *Notes on a Cellar-Book*, but of little else. The stream of the delightful cookery books—decorative, readable, practical—that nowadays fill shelf upon shelf of the gourmet's library, was then little more than a trickle, let alone coursing in full spate. Mrs. Ross's bantling was, so far as this country was concerned, something of a pioneer. Even in France, so infinitely more food-conscious than the British Isles, Brillat-Savarin, although sprung from an earlier century than Mrs. Beeton, was still the Frenchman's and Frenchwoman's unquestioned oracle on culinary taste and etiquette.

It says much for the intrinsic merit of Mrs. Ross's unassuming little book, now entering upon its seventh decade, that it should have achieved a viability in the literature of gastronomy hitherto attained only by the giants. But quite a number of contributory causes may explain this phenomenon. An obvious one is the perennial appeal of Italy to the peoples of the British Isles—an appeal promoted by the English humanists of the Renaissance; powerfully stimulated by the nobility and gentry of the eighteenth and early nineteenth centuries, who lumbered south in their coaches on the Grand Tour to return with acres of paintings and tons of statuary for the stocking of their Palladian mansions; and since then maintained by the innumerable travellers of all ages and classes who delight to follow less pompously in their trail.

Another reason is the British people's growing interest in intelligent eating already referred to. A third, surely, is the fact that Janet Ross's recipes were those actually in use in her beloved Poggio Gherardo, that fascinating Trecento villa (in the Italian sense of 'villa') outside Florence with its echoes of Boccaccio and the telling of the tales of the Decameron. And then there is the personality of the authoress herself.

Janet Duff Gordon, afterwards Janet Ross, was born in 1842 and died in 1927; she was the daughter of the Lady Duff Gordon who wrote the celebrated *Letters from Egypt* and grand-daughter of John Austin, the jurist. Her youth was spent in a literary circle, and she is the Rose Jocelyn of Meredith's *Evan Harrington*. On her marriage to Henry Ross, a man more than twenty years her senior who had helped Henry Layard with his excavations at Nimrud, she and her husband settled in Tuscany, where she came to be regarded by some of her contemporaries as a somewhat formidable person. Even as a child she had been unusually strong-minded and she once refused a request to tie Tennyson's shoe-lace. She could certainly be alarming if roused, with her determined jaw, white hair and beetling black brows; her feud with Ouida has passed into the social history of the nineteenth-century Florence and, somewhat one-sidedly, into Ouida's *roman à clef, Friendship*. Yet she could be approachable by the young, as I, at least, found her to be.

For all too long, however, the *Leaves* have been out of print; and it is with a nice appropriateness that this new and long-awaited re-issue should be edited by Janet Ross's great-great-nephew, by profession a restaurateur. She, who produced at Poggio Gherardo not only books but a rather special vermouth, will appreciate that partnership from the Elysian fields.

HARRY LUKE

Preface to the original edition

The innate love of change in man is visible even in the kitchen. Not so very long ago soup was an exception in English houses—almost a luxury. A dish of vegetables—as a dish and not an adjunct to meat—was a still greater rarity; and even now plain-boiled potatoes, peas, cabbages, etc., are the rule. When we read of the dishes, fearfully and wonderfully made, in the old Italian *novelle*, we wonder whence the present Italians got their love of vegetables and maccheroni.

Sacchetti tells us that in the fourteenth century a baked goose, stuffed with garlic and quinces, was considered an exquisite dish; and when the gonfalonier of Florence gave a supper to a famous doctor, he put before him the stomach of a calf, boiled partridges, and pickled sardines. Gianfigliazzi's cook sent up a roasted crane to his master as a delicacy, says Boccaccio; and a dish of leeks cooked with spices appears as a special dish in the rules of the chapter of San Lorenzo when the canons messed together. Old Laschi, author of that delightful book *L'Osservatore Fiorentino*, moralises on the ancient fashion of cooking in his pleasant rather prosy way: 'It would not seem that the senses should be subjected to fashion; and yet such is the case. The perfumes, once so pleasing, musk, amber, and benzoin, now excite convulsions; sweet wines, such as Pisciancio, Verdea, Montalcino, and others mentioned by Redi in his dithyrambic, are now despised; and instead of the heavy dishes of olden times, light and elegant ones are in vogue. Whoever characterised man as a laughing animal ought rather to have called him a variable and inconstant one.'

The dinner which set all Siena laughing for days, given to a favourite of Pius II by a Sienese who substituted wild geese for peacocks, after cutting off their beaks and feet, and coloured his jelly with poisonous ingredients, forms the subject of one of Pulci's tales:—

'Meanwhile it was ordered that hands should be washed, and Messer Goro was seated at the head of the table, and then other courtiers who had accompanied him; and they ate many tarts of good almond paste as a beginning. Then was brought to Messer Goro the dish on which were the peacocks without beaks, and a fellow was told to carve them. He not being used to such office gave himself vast trouble to pluck them,* but did it with so little grace that he filled the room and all the table with feathers, and the eyes, the mouth, the nose, and the ears of Messer Goro, and of them all. They, perceiving that it was from want of knowledge, held their peace, and took a mouthful here and there of other dishes so as not to disturb the order of the feast. But they were always swallowing dry feathers. Falcons and hawks would have been convenient that evening. When this pest had been removed many other roasts were brought, but all most highly seasoned with cumin. Everything would however have been pardoned if at the last an error had not been committed, which out of sheer folly nearly cost Messer Goro and those with him their lives. Now you must know that the master of the house and his councillors, in order to do honour to his guest, had ordered a dish of jelly. They wanted, as is the fashion in Florence and elsewhere, to have the arms of the Pope and of Messer Goro with many ornaments on it; so they used orpiment, white and red lead, verdigris, and other horrors, and set this before Messer

_____
*Peacocks were skinned, not plucked, before cooking, and the skin with the feathers was put on to the roasted bird, and the tail opened out before placing the dish on the table. The "fellow" ought to have cut the stitches and drawn off the skin, instead of plucking the feathers.

Goro as a choice and new thing. And Messer Goro and his companions ate willingly of it to take the bitter taste of the cumin and the other strange dishes out of their mouths, thinking, as is the custom in every decent place, that they were all coloured with saffron, milk of sweet almonds, the juices of herbs, and such like. And in the night it was just touch and go that some of them did not stretch out their legs. Messer Goro especially suffered much anguish from both head and stomach. . . .'

A company of Lombard pastrycooks came to Tuscany in the sixteenth century, and introduced fine pastry into Florence. We find the first mention of it in Berni's *Orlando Innamorato*, where it is mentioned among the choice viands. Laschi says, 'the epoch of Charles V is the greatest of modern times, for the culture of the spirit induced the culture of the body.' But he does not mention vegetables or herbs at all. For them we must go back to the ancients. Bitterly did the Israelites, when wandering in the desert, regret 'the cucumbers and the melons we did eat in Egypt'; though old Gerarde says, 'they yield to the body a cold and moist nourishment, and that very little, and the same not good.' Gerarde is however hard to please, for he says of egg-plants, under the old English name of Raging or Mad Apples, 'doubtless these apples have a mischievous qualitie, the use whereof is utterly to be forsaken.'

Fennel, dedicated to St. John, was believed to make the lean fat and to give the weak strength, while the root pounded with honey was considered a remedy against the bites of mad dogs. If lettuce be eaten after dinner it cures drunkenness; but Pope says:—

> If your wish be rest,
> Lettuce and cowslip wine, *probatum est*.

Sorrel is under the influence of Venus, and Gerarde declares that also 'the carrot serveth for love matters; and Orpheus, as Pliny writeth, said that the use hereof winneth love.' Flowers of rosemary, rue, sage, marjoram, fennel, and quince preserve youth; worn over the heart they give gaiety. Rosemary is an herb of the sun, while Venus first raised sweet marjoram, therefore young married couples are crowned with it in Greece. While

> He that eats sage in May
> Shall live for aye.

Sweet basil is often worn by the Italian maidens in their bosoms, as it is supposed to engender sympathy, and borage makes men merry and joyful.

JANET ROSS

Conversion tables

OVEN TEMPERATURES

Cool and very cool	200°F–300°F	¼–2 regulo setting
Moderate	300°F–375°F	2–5 regulo setting
Moderate to hot	375°F–400°F	6 regulo setting
Hot	400°F–475°F	6–9 regulo setting

LIQUID MEASURES

1 Litre = 1¾ pints
2 pts approx. 1.15 litres
1 pt. approx. 0.57 litre
½ pt. approx. 0.28 litre
¼ pt. approx. 0.14 litre

WEIGHTS

1 Kilo = 2 lb. 3 oz.
1 oz. approx. 28 gr.
2 oz. approx. 56 gr.
3 oz. approx. 84 gr.
4 oz. approx. 112 gr.
5 oz. approx. 142 gr.
6 oz. approx. 170 gr.
8 oz. approx. 227 gr.
12 oz. approx. 240 gr.
1 lb. approx. 453 gr.
1½ lbs. approx. 686 gr.
2 lbs. approx. 906 gr.

LEAVES
FROM OUR
TUSCAN
KITCHEN

Globe Artichokes
Carciofi

The globe artichoké is bred from the cardoon. In Italy there are two main types, the Moretti which are small and the Romani which are large and spiny.

They are eaten on the continent when half grown, the reason being that the leaves are more tender and the choke has not developed. In Italy the season is winter and spring. In England the most usual type grown is the larger spiny artichoke but far superior is the Gros Vert de Laon which is small and can be eaten whole.

1

The usual care must be taken in buying artichokes, that they are young and fresh and that they have not developed too much choke. They quickly lose their juice once they have been cut, which toughens the fibres in the leaves.

1 Carciofi Bolliti

Boiled artichokes; hot with Hollandaise sauce or cold with a special dressing

---

Cut off the stalks, pull off the outer leaves and trim the bases of

six large artichokes

Cut off, too, the top third of the artichoke which is inedible. Put them into plenty of

boiling salted water—

the base of the artichoke downwards. Cook for about twenty minutes or until the base is soft to the point of a small knife. If over-cooked they will lose their nutty flavour. Remove and drain well if they are to be served hot; or refresh in cold water and then drain if to be served cold. Once cooked they will not keep more than a day

If they are being served hot, prepare the following Hollandaise sauce while the artichokes are cooking:

Melt, but do not over-heat	6 oz. butter

Beat over hot water together with and	4 egg yolks juice of $\frac{1}{2}$ a lemon a small pinch of basil

Beat the egg yolks and lemon until creamy and thickening. Then remove from the hot water and stir in the butter slowly and thoroughly. If it is not as thick as thick cream, return to the hot water and beat a while longer.

Serve the artichokes on a napkin surrounding a pot of the sauce

If they are to be served cold, prepare the following vinaigrette, taking care to use the best olive oil

In a basin put	a pinch of salt and pepper a pinch of chopped marjoram and a teaspoon of French mustard
Stir in	2 tablespoons wine vinegar
and then	6 tablespoons olive oil
Mix well	

Serve the artichokes on a bed of lettuce surrounding a pot of the sauce. If fresh marjoram is available, put a small sprig in the top of each artichoke.

Globe Artichokes/*Carciofi*

2 *Carciofi alla Franchese*

Small peeled artichokes boiled in water and oil and finished with lemon

Here is one of the finest ways of eating artichokes

Trim the bases and cut off almost half the tops of

twelve young small artichokes

Pull off about three layers of the leaves until only the light green tender ones are left. Cut them into quarters, putting them into a basin of cold water as they are prepared. Then put them into an open pan, barely covered with

boiling water with 6 tablespoons of good olive oil salt and twelve roughly crushed peppercorns

Boil until the water has evaporated and add the

juice of a lemon

Serve hot or cold with a sprinkling of chopped parsley.

3   *Carciofi all'Italiana*

Hot, boiled artichokes with a cold sauce Tartare

Trim the bases and the tops of	**six large artichokes**
Boil them in salted water for about twenty minutes or until the point of a knife sinks into the base. Drain and serve at once on a napkin with the following sauce:	
Chop, very, very finely or liquidise	**2 anchovies** **a small onion or shallot** **3 sprigs of tarragon** **a tablespoon of capers**
Then add	**1 tablespoon wine vinegar**
And mix in	**2 egg yolks**
Finally blend in until it thickens, like a mayonnaise.	**6 tablespoons olive oil**

4   *Carciofi alla panna*

Small artichokes cooked in stock which is reduced, finished
with cream and lemon juice

Trim the bases and cut off almost half the top of	**twelve young artichokes**
Pull off the outer leaves until only the tender light green ones are left. Put the artichokes into cold water as they are prepared	
Put them into an open pan, barely cover them with stock, with a little salt and pepper and boil fast until the stock has all but gone. Shake in	**¼ pint of cream**
Let it bubble and thicken a moment on the stove. Remove the pan from the stove and stir in	**the juice of a lemon**
Serve in little pots with chopped parsley.	

5   *Cariofi fritti*

Small artichokes, dipped in light batter and deep fried,
served with lemon or tomato and garlic sauce

Trim the bases and cut off one
third of the tops of

twelve young artichokes

Pull off the outer leaves and
cut across into about four
slices, putting them into a
basin of cold water as you do
them

Make the following batter:

Form a well, add

**2 tablespoons (heaped)
flour
1 egg yolk**

and

**1 tablespoon olive oil
pepper and salt**

Mix and start stirring in the
flour, adding about

½ cup water

Until the batter is like thick
cream

Let it rest while you beat up
the

white of one egg

Fold this into the batter
Heat two or three inches of oil
in a deep pan until it begins to
smoke. Dip the pieces of
artichoke into the batter, drain

for a moment and fry in the oil
until golden.

Serve with quarters of lemon
or the following sauce:

Grate	$\frac{1}{2}$ an onion
into a pan with	2 tablespoons olive oil
add	a good pinch chopped basil
	parsley
and	1 crushed clove of garlic

Stew for a few minutes then stir in	twelve sliced tomatoes

or a tin of tomatoes, season with	salt and pepper

and boil until creamy.

6   *Cariofi farciti*

Small artichokes boiled, stuffed with ham, chicken and
cream, sprinkled with cheese and baked or grilled

Trim the bases and cut off one third of the tops of	twelve young artichokes

Boil in salted water for ten
minutes, drain and remove the
outside leaves until only the
light green ones are left. Make

a well in the centre of each one and liberally fill with the following mixture:

4 oz. ham and the pickings of a chicken (or about the same quantity as of minced ham)

Stir in

**2 tablespoons cream
chopped parsley
salt, pepper and nutmeg**

Put the artichokes into a well-buttered oven-proof dish, sprinkle with grated Parmesan and bake in a very hot oven or under the grill for 10–15 minutes. Serve at once.

7 _Carciofi alla Barigoule_

Large artichokes braised with pork, mushrooms and white wine

Trim the bases and cut off half the tops of

6 large artichokes

Boil for ten minutes, refresh in cold water and drain again. Remove the choke and fill with the following stuffing

**2 oz. minced pork
1 oz. minced bacon
1 small onion, chopped**

Stew these in a pan without colour, add

**a little olive oil
8 oz. chopped
mushrooms
salt and pepper**

Cook for five minutes, stirring from time to time

Tie a rasher of bacon round each artichoke with string, put in an oven-proof dish with oil, fry lightly. Add a glass of white wine, the same of stock, cover and braise for just under an hour in a moderate oven. Remove the string and serve with the juices.

Asparagus

Asparagi

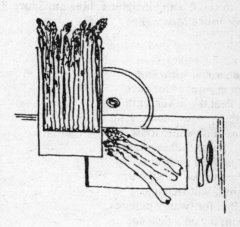

Of the many varieties grown in Italy, the commonest is the purple Genoa asparagus, in season from February through March into April.

It is a vegetable that should be simply served, but not one that is simple to cook. Having a woody stem and tender tip, it is easy to under- or over-cook it. Nor are the tinned asparagus recommended as an easy way out; being necessarily soaked in liquid for some time, they have little texture or flavour. (The best I have found to be the large white Argenteuils.)

Freshness is always important, not least with asparagus whose stems become woodier the longer they have been picked. The white stalks can be used for a soup.

1 Asparagi

Asparagus; cold with vinaigrette; hot with Sauce Beurre Fondu or Sauce Mousseline

To be generous, allow one pound of asparagus for each person. Peel the lower white part with a potato peeler. Trim the bases and tie into loose bundles. Stand them upright in a deep pan and pour over boiling water, leaving the tips uncovered. Salt well and cover. Boil for twenty minutes and drain; lay on a dish and serve hot or refresh carefully in cold water and drain again, if they are to be served cold.

Sauce Vinaigrette
(enough for six people)
In a bowl, put

a pinch of salt and pepper
a pinch of sugar
grated nutmeg
the juice of $1\frac{1}{2}$ lemons
6 tablespoons good olive oil

Mix thoroughly together and
serve with the cold asparagus

Beurre Fondu
In a small frying pan, put

**6 oz. salted butter
a pinch of ground pepper
1 tablespoon cream**

Heat, shaking the pan until the
butter and cream emulsifies.
Serve at once with the
asparagus

Sauce Mousseline
Melt, but do not over-heat

6 oz. butter

Beat over hot water

**4 egg yolks
juice of $\frac{1}{2}$ a lemon
1 egg white
salt and pepper**

Beat well until fluffy and
thickening. Remove the pan
from the water and stir in the
butter slowly and thoroughly.
Return to the pan, still beating
until it is almost setting.
Remove from the fire and fold
in

**a heaped tablespoon of
whipped cream**

Serve in a bowl with the hot
asparagus

2 *Asparagi alla Wilhelmina*

Asparagus with a slightly piquant butter sauce

Peel the white part of five or
six pounds of asparagus. Tie
loosely into bundles and trim
the bases. Put into a deep pan
and pour boiling water in up to
the tips. Salt well and boil for
twenty minutes. Drain and
arrange in a long dish.

Meanwhile prepare the following sauce: Melt in a frying pan	**4 oz. butter**
Mix in	**1 level tablespoon flour**
Cook for a minute then, stir in	**$\frac{1}{2}$ pint chicken broth** **2 bay leaves** **chopped parsley** **juice of $\frac{1}{2}$ an onion** **salt and pepper**
Bring to the boil and simmer for five minutes. Take the pan from the stove and whisk in	**3 egg yolks** **juice of $\frac{1}{2}$ a lemon**

Serve over the asparagus.

3 *Asparagi alla Parmigiana*

Asparagus with a butter and grated Parmesan sauce, finished under the grill

Cut off the green tips from four pounds of asparagus. Put into boiling salted water and cook for ten to fifteen minutes. Place in a dish and pour over them the following sauce:

Put into a frying pan

**4 oz. butter
2 oz. grated Parmesan
2 tablespoons strong stock
ground pepper and nutmeg**

Stir until the sauce bubbles. Remove from the stove and add

2 beaten egg yolks

Sprinkle with more grated Parmesan and colour quickly under the grill.

4 *Asparagi alla crema*

Asparagus with butter, cream and roast split almonds

Cut the white stalks off five
pounds asparagus and boil the
green tips in boiling salted
water for ten to fifteen
minutes. (Reserve the white
stalks for soup.)

Drain carefully, put into a
shallow dish and pour over
them the following sauce:

Into a frying-pan put   **4 oz. butter**
and   **2 tablespoons cream**

Stir until mixture bubbles, add   **juice of $\frac{1}{2}$ a lemon**
                                  ground pepper
                                  3 oz. roast split almonds

5 *Asparagi all'Italiana*

Asparagus tips with coddled eggs and cream

Cut off the green tips of three
pounds of asparagus (reserve
the white stalks for soup). Boil
in salted water for ten to
fifteen minutes and drain
carefully. Arrange the
asparagus tips in ramekins

Break **2 eggs over them**

Season with **salt and pepper**
and **chopped chives (if
available)**

Pour over **a tablespoon cream**

Pour a little hot water into the
bottom of a roasting tray, put
in the egg-dishes, cover with
another tray and bake in a hot
oven for about five minutes
until the eggs are set. They can
also be cooked in a pan with
water over a gentle flame on
top of the stove.

6 *Asparagi ai gamberi*

Asparagus with prawns and lemon mayonnaise

Cut the green tips off four
pounds of asparagus. Boil in
salted water for ten to fifteen
minutes and drain carefully.
Arrange flat on a dish

Pour over a **squeeze of lemon**
2 tablespoons of oil
salt, pepper and nutmeg

Allow to cool

Peel two pounds of large
prawns and prepare the
following sauce mayonnaise:

Put in a bowl **3 egg yolks**
salt and pepper
grated rind $\frac{1}{2}$ a lemon

Stir and mix in slowly **$\frac{1}{2}$ pint olive oil**

Then add **the juice of the whole**
lemon

Put the sauce in a pot, in the
middle of a large dish, arrange
the prawns round the pot and
the asparagus round the
prawns.

Beetroot

∽

Barbabietole

How to boil beetroot

The smaller the beetroot, the sweeter and juicier they are.
Wash them, taking care not to break the skin which will let
the juice out in the cooking.

Put them in a pan in cold water and bring to the boil. For
small ones, boil for an hour; larger ones for two hours.

Place them in cold water for five minutes and then rub
off the skin. Use as required.

1 *Barbabietole alla panna*

Beetroot in cream

Boil twelve small white or red
beetroot. Cut into dice and
pour over the following sauce:

Melt in a saucepan	$\frac{1}{2}$ oz. butter
add	$\frac{1}{2}$ oz. flour

Cook for a few minutes

Then stir in
$\frac{1}{2}$ pint single cream
salt and pepper
chopped chives or spring
onions

Bring to the boil, stirring all
the time, and cook gently for a
few minutes.

2 *Barbabietole alla Lionese*

Beetroot baked with onions and milk

Slice ten small boiled beetroot
into a basin

Slice
and cook them in
add

2 onions
2 oz. butter
$\frac{1}{2}$ oz. flour
$\frac{1}{2}$ pint milk
salt, sugar and pepper

Bring the sauce to the boil,
stirring. Mix in the basin with
the beetroot and lay in an
oven-dish. Pour a little cream
over and bake in a hot oven.

3   *Beetroot Salad*

Slice twelve small cooked
beetroot onto a dish. Sprinkle
with tarragon vinegar, salt and
coarsely ground pepper

Leave for a few hours and
when serving, add olive oil or
cream.

4   *Barbabietole alla Parmigiana*

Small beetroots, baked whole with cream and Parmesan
cheese

Peel eighteen very small
cooked beetroot and put them
into a buttered oven-dish

Over them sprinkle

    salt and pepper
    $\frac{1}{2}$ pint single cream
    chopped chives
    2 oz. grated Parmesan
    a few small knobs of
    butter

Bake in a hot oven and serve,
perhaps, with hot tongue.

Broad Beans

Fave

Beans and peas must be eaten young, for with age the sugar
turns to starch and the skin toughens. Broad beans are best
eaten when they are no bigger than a finger nail and the
pod, which is usually no longer than four inches at this
stage, can be cut and eaten as well. (See *alla Turca*.)

All the following recipes use the cooking liquid as part of
the sauce; this preserves more of the flavour and nutriment.
If the vegetable is found to be cooked before enough of the
liquid has evaporated, drain the vegetable into another pan,
boil the liquid fiercely and finish as the recipe requires.

1 *Fave al burro*

Broad beans cooked with ham

Shell three pounds young
broad beans. Put them in a

saucepan with

a thick slice of ham
a stick of celery
parsley
3 cloves
twelve peppercorns
pinch of salt and a bayleaf

Just cover with boiling water
and boil fiercely for ten to
fifteen minutes until the beans
are cooked and the liquid has
almost evaporated

Remove the celery and other
seasonings, chop up the ham
and return it to the beans and
stir in

2 oz. butter

2 *Fave alla Turca*

Take three pounds of young
beans no more than four inches
long.

Cut each pod into three,
putting them into cold water as
you cut them

Boil in salted water for ten to
fifteen minutes, drain and mix
in

2 oz. butter, salt and
pepper

3 *Fave al vino*

Shell	**3 lb. young broad beans**
Put in a pan and	**1 oz. butter** **½ an onion finely chopped**
When cooked stir in	**1 oz. flour**
Then add the beans, and	**a sprig of chopped marjoram salt and pepper 1 teaspoon sugar ¼ pint cheap white wine**

Just cover with stock and boil
fiercely until cooked.

4 *Fave alla Romana*

Shell three pounds of broad
beans

Stew in	**1 chopped onion** **2 tablespoons olive oil**
Add	**a large sprig chopped sage**
and	**1 dessertspoon tomato purée**

Just cover with boiling water
and boil fiercely until cooked
and the juice has reduced.
Serve hot or cold.

Broccoli spears

The season for good broccoli spears in England (early Spring) is short. They are picked when they are the size of a small cauliflower, fist size, with tightly bunched heads. They can be cooked whole when very small, or split into smaller heads with a small knife, prior to cooking.

They should be eaten simply, like asparagus.

1 *Broccoli al burro*

Take off most of the leaves and some of the stalk from four pounds of broccoli spears. Put them in plenty of boiling salted water and cook for about twenty minutes, taking care not to break the heads. Drain carefully and put into a serving dish

Pour over
sprinkle with

4 oz. butter
salt and rough ground
pepper

2 Broccoli alla Parmigiana

Prepare and cook four pounds
of broccoli in boiling salted
water for about twenty
minutes. Drain them carefully
and lay them in an oven dish.
Pour over the following sauce:

In a saucepan, put	$\frac{1}{2}$ oz. butter
Heat and add	$\frac{1}{2}$ oz. flour
Cook for a few minutes, then add	$\frac{1}{2}$ pint milk salt, pepper and nutmeg
Bring to the boil, stirring well, then add	4 oz. grated Parmesan

Cook for a few minutes. Pour
the sauce over the broccoli.
Sprinkle with more grated
cheese and bake in a hot oven.

3 *Broccoli all'Olandese*

Prepare and cook four pounds
of broccoli spears for twenty
minutes, drain carefully and
place on a serving dish

Meanwhile prepare the
following sauce:

Melt, but do not over-heat   **6 oz. butter**

Beat over hot water   **4 egg yolks**

Together with   **juice of half a lemon
                                    a small pinch cayenne**

Beat the eggs until creamy and
thickening, remove from the
hot water and stir in the butter
slowly and thoroughly. Serve
with the broccoli.

Broccoli spears   27

Brussels sprouts

Cavolini di Brusselle

1   *Cavolini di Brusselle al limone*

Wash two pounds of very small brussels sprouts and cut off the outside leaves. Boil in plenty of boiling salted water for ten minutes until cooked through. Drain and toss in a pan with

the juice of a lemon
2 oz. butter
salt and a good sprinkling of coarse ground pepper.

2 *Cavolini di Brusselle alla Milanese*

Prepare two pounds of very small brussels sprouts and cook them in plenty of boiling salted water for about ten minutes. Drain them well

Heat
and
in a frying pan

1 oz. butter
2 tablespoons olive oil

Add the sprouts and fry over a rather fierce heat, tossing frequently. When they are beginning to brown, add

1 oz. breadcrumbs
1 oz. grated Parmesan

Continue to cook, taking care that the sprouts do not break up. Serve at once.

Cabbage

Cavolo

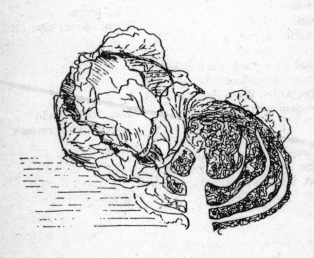

Cabbage is, perhaps, the most abused of all vegetables. If it is overcooked, it is quite useless for taste and food value. My publisher, Jock Murray, maintains that drinking cabbage water is excellent for general health and particularly for rheumatism. Cabbage, at any rate, deserves proper attention. Its cooking time will vary according to the type of cabbage, how fresh it is and how much stalk the leaves have. The general rule is to cook cabbage in plenty of boiling water, so that the water reboils quickly once the cabbage is added; alternatively it can be cooked (more usually the white or red cabbage) without any water at all.

1 Cavolo al burro

Cut two large cabbages into six segments each, and cut off most of the stalk. Wash in cold water. Throw into boiling water with salt for ten to fifteen minutes, according to the type of cabbage and how stalky the leaves are. Drain, at once, and mix in a pan with melted butter, salt and pepper.

2 Cavolo alla panna

Cut one large white cabbage into four and remove the stalks. Shred the leaves across, not too finely. Wash in cold water. Put into a pan of boiling salted water for ten minutes, drain well. Return it to the pan and add

½ pint thin cream
salt, ground pepper and nutmeg
1 dessertspoon grated horseradish

Cover the pan with a lid and finish cooking gently, stirring the cabbage from time to time. If the cabbage has made more juice, remove the lid, when nearly cooked and boil fiercely to reduce.

3 Cavolo al forno

Cut one large white cabbage (or Savoy) into six segments and cut off most of the stalk. Wash in cold water. Blanch in boiling salted water for ten minutes, drain and refresh under cold water. Drain well

Butter a shallow oven dish, arrange the segments of cabbage in it and add

salt and ground pepper
½ pint stock
4 oz. butter in nuts

The stock should cover about a third of the cabbage. Cover with greaseproof paper and braise in a fairly hot oven for about half an hour, until cooked. Salt pork, ham, sausages or garlic sausage added before the cabbage goes in the oven, makes a meal in itself.

4   *Cavolo fritto*

Cut one large white cabbage
into four and remove the stalk.
Shred the leaves across, not
too finely. Blanch in boiling
salted water for five minutes,
drain well. Return to the pan
with

4 oz. butter
salt and cayenne
4 crushed juniper berries
2 tablespoons vinegar

Toss over a gentle fire until
cooked.

5   *Cavolo stufato*

Prepare and blanch a white
cabbage as in the last recipe.
Drain it. Meanwhile cook
in
add

1 chopped onion
4 tablespoons olive oil
8 chopped tomatoes (or a
tin)
salt and pepper
pinch of mixed herbs

Add the cabbage to the sauce,
cover with a lid and finish
cooking.

Cabbage/*Cavolo*

6 *Cavolo alla Fiamminga*

Cut two small red cabbages
into four and remove the stalk.
Shred not too finely and
blanch in boiling salted water
for five minutes. Drain well
and return to the pan with

**4 oz. butter
a grated onion
2 oz. chopped lean bacon
2 cloves
bay leaf, salt and pepper**

Cook gently for about twenty
minutes until cooked and
remove the bay leaf and
cloves.

7 *Cavolo alla Tedesca*

Cut two small red cabbages
into four and remove the stalk.
Shred, not too finely, and
blanch in boiling salted water
for five minutes. Drain well
and return to the pan with

**4 oz. butter
salt and pepper
sprinkling of caraway
seeds
2 tablespoons wine
vinegar
1 grated onion**

Finish cooking over a gentle
heat for about twenty minutes.

8 _Cavolo ripieno_

Cabbage leaves stuffed with spinach and mushrooms

Cut off the main stalk of a
large green cabbage (preferably
Savoy), and remove the leaves.
Blanch the leaves in boiling
salted water for five minutes
and drain well. Cut any thick
stalk from the leaves and fill
with the following:

$\frac{1}{2}$ lb. chopped cooked
spinach
$\frac{1}{4}$ lb. chopped cooked
mushrooms
3 egg yolks
4 oz. fresh breadcrumbs
salt and pepper
2 oz. grated cheese

Wrap this mixture in the leaves
and braise in stock and butter
in a moderate oven for about
half an hour.

Capsicums (Peppers)

Peperoni

Peeling peppers is by no means easy, particularly in England where the peppers are not freshly picked. They can be plunged into boiling fat for a minute but the result is not always satisfactory. The skins, however, may be left on, providing the peppers are as firm and as fresh as possible. It is left to the discretion of the cook whether they be peeled or not.

1 *Peperoni alla Spagnuola*

Cut six peppers (red, green
and yellow, if possible) in half
and remove the seeds. Cut into
thick strips

Heat, in a deep frying pan
in it, fry

$\frac{1}{4}$ **pint olive oil**
2 sliced onions
2 large cloves garlic
(chopped)
the sliced peppers

and

When almost cooked, add

8 chopped tomatoes (or a
tin)
salt and pepper

Finish cooking for another ten
minutes, until the peppers are
still slightly crisp. This can be
eaten hot or cold.

2 *Peperoni farciti*

Peppers filled with chicken, rice and thyme and braised

Cut off the stalk end of six
large peppers and remove the
seeds. Cook in boiling salted
water for ten minutes; drain
and fill with the following
risotto:

Capsicums(Peppers)/*Peperoni*   37

| Fry, in olive oil
add | 1 chopped onion
½ lb. chopped cooked chicken
4 oz. rice |

| Fry for a few minutes then add | ½ pint chicken stock
chopped thyme
salt and pepper |

Cook for about 12 minutes until the rice begins to swell, then fill the peppers three-quarters full with rice and stock

Put the peppers, open end up, carefully in a dish, sprinkle with olive oil and stock and bake in a hot oven for twenty to thirty minutes. Serve hot or cold.

3   Peperoni farciti

Peppers with pork, herbs and cheese

| Cut six peppers in half and remove the seeds. Fill the halves with the following stuffing: | 1 lb. pork sausage meat
2 eggs
salt, pepper and nutmeg
chopped chives
chopped marjoram |
| On each pepper place | a thick slice of Emmenthal cheese |

Put them in an oven dish with pieces of butter and a little stock and bake in a moderate oven for about half an hour.

4 Peperoni fritti

Deep-fried slices of peppers with tomato and basil sauce

Cut six peppers in half and remove the seeds. Cut the peppers into half again lengthwise and dip them into this batter:

Make a well in
add

2 tablespoons flour
1 egg yolk
1 tablespoon olive oil

Mix and start stirring in the flour, adding

3 tablespoons water
a pinch of salt and pepper

until the batter is like thick cream

Deep fry the slices of pepper in this batter and serve with the following sauce:

Fry, in olive oil

when cooked add

1 chopped onion (small)
1 clove garlic (small)
8 chopped tomatoes (or a tin)
salt and pepper
1 teaspoon chopped basil

Cardoons

❧

Cardi

Cardoons are the top stalks of thistle artichokes, delicious in flavour. They should be grown with the earth piled high so that the stalks remain white.

1   *Cardi al burro*

Peel three pounds of cardoons
and cut them in two
lengthwise, putting them into
cold water as they are
prepared, to keep them white.
Cook in boiling salted water
for ten to fifteen minutes, drain
and toss in butter and a little
more salt and pepper.

2 Cardi in umido

Peel three pounds of cardoons
and cut them into two inch
lengths. Blanch in salted water
for five minutes. Drain, and
dip in flour. Fry in olive oil
until brown and cooked. Put
into a serving dish, sprinkle
with lemon juice and cheese.

Carrots

∽

Carote

1 *Carote all'aceto*

Carrots with vinegar

Peel six large carrots, cut them
into four lengthways and
remove some of the hard
centre core. Cut into inch
pieces, put into a shallow
saucepan and just cover with

cold water
2 bay leaves
3 tablespoons wine
vinegar
$\frac{1}{2}$ minced onion
3 crushed juniper berries
a little salt and pepper

Bring to the boil and boil
fiercely until the liquid has
almost gone and the carrots
are cooked. Sprinkle with
chopped parsley and serve hot
or cold.

2 *Carote al vermouth*

Glazed carrots in vermouth

Wash and peel six large carrots. Quarter them lengthways, cut out the hard centre and dice the remainder

Put the carrots into a thick pan with
add a pinch of

2 oz. butter
salt and pepper and sugar

Set the carrots in the butter for three minutes

Then add

1 wineglass cheap white vermouth

Cover the pan and stew the carrots rather gently, shaking the pan from time to time. Add a little water if the carrots get dry. When the carrots are tender (about twenty-five minutes) remove the lid and bubble up the liquid until it thickens to a syrup. Empty into a dish and sprinkle with parsley. The syrupy effect of this dish is not always so easy to achieve due, I think to how much moisture there is in the carrots. For the final stage, when the carrots are tender (if dry) sprinkle lightly with sugar

Carrots/*Carote*

and add a little more vermouth
and toss over a good flame to
caramelise. This is a good dish
with pork and lamb.

3   *Carote alla Parmigiana*

Carrots and celery with Parmesan

Wash and peel six large carrots
and three outside sticks of
celery. Quarter the carrots
lengthwise, cut out the hard
centre and dice the remainder.
Dice the celery and put both
into a pan. Just cover with
cold water, add chicken
bouillon to season and bring to
the boil. Simmer until tender.
Strain the carrots and celery,
keeping the cooking liquor. Put
the carrots and celery into a
dish and make a veloute sauce
with the stock:

In a saucepan melt	**1 oz. butter**
add and mix in	**1 oz. flour**

Cook the roux and add the
stock, bring to the boil and
reduce until the sauce is the
thickness of double cream

Then stir in	**1 oz. grated Parmesan**
and	**1 oz. grated cheddar**

Pour the sauce over the carrots and celery sprinkle with Parmesan cheese and bake in a hot oven for ten minutes (this can be prepared in advance and baked when required for fifteen to twenty minutes).

4 *Carote alla casalinga*

Top, tail and wash three pounds of very young carrots. Put them into a pan with cold water and salt. Bring to the boil and half cook for five minutes. Drain them and return to the pan with

4 oz. butter
salt, pepper and sugar
pinch of rosemary

Cover with a lid and stew over a gentle flame until cooked. Then add, away from the stove,

3 tablespoons stock
juice of $\frac{1}{2}$ a lemon
3 egg yolks, beaten

Shake the pan until the sauce thickens, put into a dish and sprinkle with chopped parsley.

5   *Carote al forno*

Trim two pounds of medium-sized carrots, scrape them and put in a pan of cold water to boil. Parboil for ten minutes, drain and lay in a buttered oven dish. Half-cover with stock, sprinkle with salt, pepper, pinch of thyme and small pieces of butter

Braise in a rather hot oven, basting from time to time, until cooked.

Cauliflower

❦

Cavolfiori

1   *Cavolfiori al burro*

The best cauliflowers have
small tightly-packed, white
heads. Trim the outside leaves
of three very small, or two
larger cauliflowers. Cut a cross
into the thick base of the stem.
Wash in cold water. Put into a
pan with plenty of cold water
and add salt and pepper. Bring
to the boil and cook carefully
for twenty or so minutes
(longer for a very large
cauliflower). Drain with care
and put on a dish in a warm
oven. Prepare a butter sauce
with:

2 oz. butter
1 tablespoon wine vinegar
or lemon
salt and coarsely ground
pepper
chopped parsley

Put the ingredients in a small
pan, let them bubble up,
without separating, and pour
over the cauliflower.

2 Cavolfiori alla Parmigiana

Trim two medium or three
very small cauliflowers and cut
a cross in the stem. Cover with
plenty of salted cold water and
boil for about twenty minutes.
Drain with care, put on to a
dish and pour over the
following cheese sauce:

Heat	**1 oz. butter**
add	**1 oz. flour**
and cook	
Add	**1 pint milk**
stir, bring to the boil and cook for a few minutes	
Add and blend	**salt and pepper**
	grated nutmeg
	2 oz. grated cheese
	1 dessertspoon french mustard

Pour the sauce over the
cauliflower, sprinkle with more
grated cheese and brown in a
very hot oven.

3 Cavolfiori fritti

Cut off the leaves of two
medium cauliflowers and cut
off the 'flowers' where they
join the main core. Put into a
pan of cold water and parboil
for ten minutes. Dip each piece
in beaten egg and breadcrumbs
and fry in half butter, half oil.
Sprinkle with grated cheese
before serving.

4 Cavolfiori alla Piemontese

'Flowers' of cauliflowers cooked with onion, anchovy and
marjoram

Remove the flowers from two
medium-sized cauliflowers and
parboil them for ten minutes.
Drain them and return to the
pan with

1 small grated onion
6 finely chopped
anchovies
1 tablespoon vinegar
$\frac{1}{4}$ pint olive oil
chopped marjoram

Cover with a lid

Cook for a few minutes and
serve hot or cold.

Celery

❧

Sedano

Choose fat heads of celery, not too long and stringy, nor brown from frost or being packed too tight. The very outside leaves and stalks can be used for soups and stocks.

1 *Sedano fritto*

Remove the outer stalks and cut off the leaves of three heads of celery. Cut into two-inch lengths and wash the pieces well in cold water. Parboil in salted water for fifteen minutes but it should still be crisp. Drain, dip in egg and breadcrumbs and fry in half butter, half oil.

2 *Sedano all'Italiana*

Celery, thyme and tomatoes

Remove the outer stalks of two
large heads of celery and cut
off the leaves. Cut into inch
lengths and wash well

Into a deep frying-pan put

$\frac{1}{4}$ pint olive oil
1 chopped onion
the pieces of celery

Fry until the celery is golden
and almost cooked, then add

$\frac{1}{2}$ pint tomato juice
salt and pepper
little chopped thyme

Cook for another few minutes
and serve.

3 *Sedano al forno*

Celery braised with ham and bay leaves

Remove the outside stalks and
cut off the green leaves of
three celery heads. Trim the
roots and cut them into four,
lengthways. Parboil in salted
water for ten minutes, drain

Celery/Sedano

and lay on a buttered oven
dish with

**6 oz. chopped ham or
bacon
coarsely ground pepper
1 pint stock (half-way up
celery)
3 bay leaves
small pieces of butter**

Cook in a rather hot oven for
twenty to thirty minutes.

4 Sedano alla Greca

Remove the outer stalks and
cut off the leaves of three
heads of celery. Cut into two-
inch lengths and wash well in
cold water. Parboil for ten
minutes in salted water, drain
and put into a deep frying pan
with

**½ pint stock
juice of a lemon
4 tablespoons olive oil
3 bay leaves
1 tablespoon coriander
seeds
a little salt and pepper**

Cook over a moderate fire
until tender and the stock has
reduced. Serve hot or cold.

Celeriac

1 Celeriac 'remoulade'

Peel a medium-sized celeriac
root with a knife, cutting away
any brown patches. Slice it on
a mandolin (or finely with a
sharp knife) and shred into
long matchsticks. Mix, at once,
with the following sauce:

In a bowl, put

2 egg yolks
1 tablespoon tarragon
vinegar
2 tablespoons french
mustard
salt and pepper

Gradually add

2 tablespoons olive oil
2 tablespoons thick cream

Chicory

⌒

Cicoria

1   *Cicoria brasata*

Braised Chicory

Wash one and a half pounds of
chicory and if they are thick,
split them down the middle
into two, three or four. Lay
them in a flat baking dish with

2 oz. butter in nuts
1 cup stock or water and
chicken bouillon
salt and pepper to taste
juice of a $\frac{1}{2}$ lemon
1 teaspoon sugar

Bring the liquid to the boil,
cover the pan and cook in a
fairly hot oven for ten minutes
with the lid and a further ten to
fifteen minutes with the lid off.
Sprinkle with chopped parsley
and serve.

2 *Cicoria con prosciutto*

Chicory and Ham

**6 very thin slices of ham
twelve pieces of cooked
chicory**

Cut the slices of ham in two
and wrap each half round the
chicory laying them in a
buttered dish. Pour over a
Sauce Mornay, sprinkle with
cheese and bake in a hot oven
for twenty minutes

Sauce Mornay
Melt
add and cook
add gradually

add

**1 oz. butter
1 oz. flour
$\frac{1}{4}$ pint milk or milk and
single cream
2 oz. grated cheddar
salt, pepper and nutmeg**

Bring to the boil, and pour
over the chicory.

3 *Tortino di cicoria*

Chicory Tart

Line a six-inch flan dish with
short pastry. Roughly chop
three pieces of cooked chicory

Lay them in the flan

In a bowl mix

2 eggs
2 oz. grated cheddar
$\frac{1}{4}$ pint milk
$\frac{1}{4}$ pint single cream
**pinch of salt, pepper and
nutmeg**

Pour the mixture over the
chicory in the flan and bake in
a moderate oven for about
thirty minutes until the cheese
and egg has set. Makes a good
simple meal with cold ham and
a green salad.

4 *Insalata di cicoria*

Chicory Salad with hazelnut dressing

Roughly chop three pieces of
chicory and put into a salad
bowl

Toss with a dressing made as
follows:

In a cup put

1 tablespoon crushed
hazelnuts
pinch of salt and pepper
pinch of sugar
1 juice of a lemon
4 oz. fluid cream

Mix the dressing thoroughly
and dress the chicory. Do not
leave the chicory too long
undressed—it will discolour.
Sprinkle with chopped parsley
and surround the bowl with
washed watercress.

Courgettes

Zucchini

Courgettes are baby marrows, easily grown, and, I would think, becoming more popular than the large marrows. The season is the summer, the end of June through to September.

Courgettes survive several days after being picked because of their high water content; and for the same reason are preferably cooked without water.

The flowers (male and female), though without marked flavour, make excellent eating. They should be prepared within a few hours of picking to prevent them wilting.

1 *Zucchini al burro*

Courgettes cooked with a little water and butter in a
covered pan

Wash two and half pounds of
small courgettes and trim off
the stems

Put them in a thick saucepan
with

**2 fluid oz. water
4 oz. butter
salt and ground pepper**

Cover with a lid and place on a
low fire, tossing the pan until
the courgettes are very nearly
soft (*al dente*)

Serve in a hot dish with plenty
of

**chopped parsley
and a squeeze of lemon**

2 *Zucchini al pomodoro*

Courgettes cooked with onion, garlic and tomatoes

Wash two and a half pounds of
courgettes and trim off the
stems. Cut them into inch

lengths and put them in a deep frying pan with

1 medium sliced onion
2 cloves garlic chopped
4 tablespoons olive oil
a little salt and pepper

Cover with a lid and stew for ten minutes, stirring from time to time. Remove the lid, turn up the heat and fry until slightly golden

Add

half a kilo tin of Italian tomatoes or
1 lb. peeled ripe tomatoes

or
add more

salt and pepper

Cook for a few moments longer only. Serve hot with roast meat or cold with fish salad.

3 *Zucchini farciti*

Courgettes stuffed with spinach and cream cheese and grilled

There are two methods for preparing the courgettes for this dish, depending on their size

If they are small, and therefore difficult to stuff, it is better to cook them in butter and a little water and then slit them ready for the stuffing. Allow four for each person as a beginning or six as a main course lunch dish

If they are larger (about six inches) trim off the stems and 'core' them carefully with an apple corer

In either case fill them with the following stuffing:

Soften in a bowl near the stove	**3 demi-sel cheeses**
Cook, for a few minutes	**1 lb. prepared spinach or a packet of frozen leaf spinach**
Refresh under cold water, squeeze dry and chop	
Add	**1 whole egg salt, pepper and nutmeg**

Mix all the above ingredients together and stuff the courgettes. (If the courgettes are cored, force the mixture in with a piping bag or small spoon)

The cooked courgettes have their cooking liquor poured over them, sprinkle them with grated Parmesan cheese and brown under the grill

The large courgettes, cored, stuffed and ready for cooking

are laid in a dish with a little
water, butter and seasoning
and baked in a moderate oven.
When cooked, sprinkle with
grated Parmesan and finish
under the grill.

4   *Fiori di Zucchini ripieni al pilaf*

A beginning dish of courgettes flowers filled with a saffron
and cayenne pilaf and deep fried, served with tomato sauce

Allow two to three flowers per
person

Fill them with the following
pilaf:

Heat in a thick pan	**2 tablespoons olive oil**
Add	**a small pinch of crushed saffron** **4 oz. patna rice** **a pinch of cayenne pepper** **1 teaspoon paprika**
Fry the ingredients without browning the rice then add	**½ pint boiling stock** **salt**

Simmer until the rice is very
nearly cooked and allow to
cool

Meanwhile, prepare the
following batter:

Put in a bowl

**2 tablespoons (heaped)
flour**

Make a well, add

**1 egg
1 tablespoon olive oil
pepper and salt**

Mix together and start stirring
in until the batter is a thickish
cream

3 tablespoons water

Dip the stuffed flowers into the
batter, drain and deep fry until
golden

Serve the following sauce
separately:

**twelve sliced tomatoes
(or a tin Italian tomatoes)**

Put in a saucepan

**1 tablespoon olive oil
½ grated onion
salt and a little sugar**

Cook until creamy and pass
through a sieve.

5 *Fiori di Zucchini ripieni di pollo*

Courgette flowers stuffed with chicken

Allow two or three flowers per
person and fill them with a
tablespoonful of the following
mixture:

Make a roux with	**1½ oz. flour** **1½ oz. butter**
Cook until sandy, add gradually	**½ pint milk** **pepper and nutmeg** **a nut of chicken bouillon**
Simmer for five minutes (the sauce should be thick) and then mix in	**4 oz. finely chopped ham** **8 oz. finely chopped cooked chicken**

Cover with greaseproof paper and allow the mixture to get cold

Dip the stuffed flowers in a batter made in the same way as in the previous recipe

Deep fry them, turning them once or twice and serve on a napkin with segments of lemon and watercress.

Cucumber

∞

Cetriolo

1 Cetriolo alla Comasca

Cut some strips of peel from a cucumber and slice the cucumber very fine on a mandolin. Arrange on a dish and sprinkle over

$\frac{1}{2}$ an onion grated (or very finely chopped)
1 tablespoon tarragon vinegar
2 tablespoons good olive oil

Allow it to 'pickle' for fifteen minutes before serving.

2   *Cetriolo condito al miele*

Cucumber with honey dressing

Cut some strips from a
cucumber, cut the cucumber
into inch pieces and then into
rather thin wedges. Pour over
the following dressing:

1 full teaspoon honey
salt and pepper
pinch chopped marjoram
2 tablespoons wine
vinegar
4 tablespoons olive oil

3   *Cetriolo al burro*

Cucumber cooked with butter, chervil and lemon

Cut strips of peel from two
cucumbers, cut the cucumbers
into two inch pieces and then
into thick wedges

Put them in a thick pan with

4 oz. butter
1 cup water
large pinch chervil

Cover with a lid and stew
gently for fifteen minutes

Meanwhile, with a very sharp
knife, cut the skin and pith
from

2 lemons

Then cut out the segments
from the dividing skin. Add the
segments of the lemons to the
cucumber, squeeze the skins
over and shake the pan over a
gentle heat

Add

2 oz. of butter in pieces

Remove from the stove and
shake again

Serve with a meat dish that is
cooked with fruit, such as
lamb basted with honey or
pork with apricots.

4   *Cetriolo alla Spagnuola*

Stuffed cucumbers, tied, and baked with onions, carrots
and thyme

Cut strips of peel from two
cucumbers. Cut the cucumbers
into two lengthways

With a teaspoon, remove some
of the seeds, the length of the
cucumber. Fill with the
following mixture and tie the

two halves together	8 oz. minced ham
	8 oz. cooked minced
	chicken or meat
	salt, pepper and nutmeg
	pinch chopped thyme
	1 egg

| In a long casserole fry in oil | 2 sliced onions |
| | 3 chopped carrots |

When almost cooked, remove	
and fry the cucumbers. Return	
the onions and carrots and add	6 halved tomatoes
	a small sprig thyme
	6 peppercorns
	a little salt

Cover the casserole and bake
in a moderate oven for half an
hour, until the cucumbers are
cooked. Remove the
cucumbers. Pass the remainder
through a sieve or Mouli.
Remove the string from the
cucumbers and pour the sauce
over them.

5   *Cetriolo alla Toscana*

Cucumber cooked with butter, cream and nutmeg

Cut strips of peel from two
cucumbers and cut into thick
slices

Put them in a pan with

4 oz. butter
1 cup water
salt and pepper

Cook over a rather gentle heat
without a lid and when nearly
cooked add

1 cup cream
$\frac{1}{2}$ nutmeg grated

Shake the pan over the fire
until the cream thickens,
empty into a dish and sprinkle
with paprika.

Egg-plant

<small>∽</small>

Melanzane

Vegetables that are foreign to England were viewed with the utmost suspicion by the medieval herbalists. Egg-plants were called 'mad' or 'raging' apples and I imagine were scarce indeed. But they have always made a colourful impact in continental market displays and are obtainable in England, more or less, all the year round. Their colour is unique among vegetables and the capacity of the flesh to absorb oil and juices makes the egg-plant valuable in a vegetable stew or cooked with spices.

1 *Melanzane fritte*

Choose three large, firm egg-plants of a smooth dark colour. Cut off the peel and stalk and cut into thick slices. Put them in a colander with a sprinkling of salt and leave for half an hour so that some of the bitter juice may escape.

Meanwhile, prepare the following batter:

In a bowl put

2 heaped tablespoons flour

Make a well, add

1 egg
salt and pepper
1 tablespoon olive oil

Star stirring in the flour and gradually add
until you have a thick, creamy consistency

3 tablespoons water

Dip the pieces of egg-plant in this and deep fry for about five minutes

Serve with a tomato sauce, made simply with

twelve sliced tomatoes
2 crushed cloves of garlic
salt and pepper
bay leaf
1 tablespoon olive oil

Cook these until creamy and
pass through a sieve.

2 *Melanzane alla griglia, Genovese*

Grilled egg-plant with a basil and garlic sauce

Peel three large egg-plants and
cut off the stalks. Cut into
thick slices, diagonally, almost
the length of the egg-plant. Put
into a colander with a
sprinkling of salt to draw out
the bitter juices

Then season with

**2 tablespoons flour
salt and coarsely ground
pepper**

Light the grill in advance,
brush the grill tray with oil.
Then dip the pieces of egg-
plant in the flour and lay them
on the grill, brush with oil.
Grill on both sides, brushing
with olive oil as they cook.
Keep in a hot oven until they
have all been grilled. Serve
with the following *pesto* sauce.
(*Pesto* can be bought in tins—
use it sparingly)

| Pound, in a mortar to a fine paste | 3 cloves of garlic
2 sprigs of basil
4 chopped walnuts |
| Gradually work in | 2 tablespoons olive oil. |

3 _Melanzane al forno_

Egg-plant cooked with tomato, garlic, breadcrumbs and Parmesan cheese

Peel three large egg-plants and cut off their stalks. Slice obliquely and put into a colander with a sprinkling of salt until the bitter juice is drawn out

| Meanwhile, peel and slice | twelve tomatoes |
| Crush over them
and make a mixture of | 3 cloves garlic
2 oz. breadcrumbs
1 grated lemon rind
2 oz. grated Parmesan |

Pour a little olive oil into the bottom of a large, fairly shallow oven dish, arrange layers of egg-plant and tomato, add a little more olive oil, press down and sprinkle with the breadcrumbs and Parmesan

Bake in a rather hot oven for
about half an hour. Serve very
hot (with, perhaps, a grilled
steak).

4 *Insalata di Melanzane*

A salad of sliced egg-plant and tomatoes, cooked in white
wine

Peel three large egg-plants and
cut off the stalks. Slice fairly
thick and leave in a colander
with a sprinkling of salt to
draw out the juices

Meanwhile peel   **twelve tomatoes**
and slice them

Heat some olive oil in a frying
pan (until very hot) and fry the
egg-plants in it, turning rather
quickly for they will easily
take colour. Keep those that
are cooked to one side, if there
are too many for one pan

Put them in the pan and pour
over   **1 glass white wine**
add   **2 cloves crushed garlic**
a little   **chopped basil**

Let it bubble and reduce and
then empty the pan over the
sliced tomatoes and arrange on
a dish when cold.

Fennel

❧

Finocchio

Bulb fennel is nowadays quite regularly imported to England, which is fortunate as it is a difficult plant to grow. The failure seems to be lack of fine weather at the moment when the plant is about to fill out, resulting in the fine feathery sprays of the herb fennel.

The bulb should be firm and white; discolouration and dryness of the outer sheathes indicate old age, which, alas, can happen with the time lapse in transport from abroad. The outer sheaths may, then, need peeling or removing. The green shoots and leaves are cut to the top of the bulb —these can be happily used as a flavouring for another dish. The flavour of fennel, cooked and uncooked varies in the same way as celery, and there are many who prefer the raw flavour. Fennel fritters, however, fried crisp and brown have a fine nutty taste and go very well with a grilled fish.

In Italy bulb fennel has many uses in a salad, very often a few slivers are mixed with the winter radish leaves or appear chopped on top of a tomato salad. In this way it is used for its crispness and as a secondary flavour. On its own it is best cut very thin and served with a pot of best oil and vinegar and seasoning, separate. This, as an accompaniment to a fine goat's cheese, both fennel and cheese being sprinkled with oil and pepper makes an excellent end to a meal.

1 *Finocchi al burro*

Fennel with butter

Trim the top shoots of four
medium-sized bulbs of fennel
and peel the outer sheaths with
a potato peeler (if white and
young, this is not necessary).
Trim the base and cut the
fennel first in half and then
each half into three or four.
Wash the segments well and
cook them in boiling salted
water (with a small piece of
lemon to keep the colour) for
about twenty minutes, until
just tender

Meanwhile melt in a casserole **1 oz. butter**
and grate into it $\frac{1}{2}$ **onion**

Strain the cooked fennel, drain
well and toss in the butter.
Sprinkle with grated Parmesan
and serve in the casserole. A
good dish to go with slices of
veal with Marsala sauce.

2 *Fritto di finocchi*

Fennel fritters with lemon

Trim three or four bulbs of
fennel and cut them first in half
and then in thin segments,
each piece held together by the
stalk

Heat the oil in the deep fryer
and make the following batter:

put the flour in a bowl and
make a well
add
and
stir in
season with

**1 tablespoon (heaped)
flour
1 egg white
1 tablespoon olive oil
$\frac{1}{2}$ cup water (tepid)
salt and pepper**

Dip the pieces of fennel
individually into the batter (the
batter should coat the fennel
but not cling in quantity to it
nor contain too much water,
which will make the batter
disintegrate in the fat)

Fry the fennel until crisp and
brown, drain and place on a
dish with a paper napkin (keep
in a warm oven while the
remainder are fried). Serve
with good-sized pieces of
lemon.

3 *Finocchi al forno*

Fried fennel with tomatoes and garlic with a crisp topping

Trim the tops and bases of four
fennel bulbs. Halve the bulbs
and cut into thin segments into
a thick shallow gratin dish (or
frying pan)

Heat
into the oil put
and

$\frac{1}{2}$ cup olive oil
1 onion thinly sliced
2 chopped cloves of garlic

Fry for a minute or two and
add the fennel, continue frying
stirring occasionally with a
wooden spoon. When the
fennel is beginning to brown
and is almost cooked add

One twelve oz. tin of
Italian peeled tomatoes,
broken up, salt and
ground pepper

Lower the heat and infuse for
five minutes

This initial cooking can be
done in advance

Sprinkle the following topping
over the fennel in the gratin

dish (or transfer into a gratin
dish from the frying-pan)

$\frac{1}{2}$ cup breadcrumbs,
roughly crushed
$\frac{1}{2}$ cup grated Parmesan
$\frac{1}{2}$ grated rind of lemon
1 chopped clove garlic

Bake in a hot oven until crisp.

French beans

Fagiolini

The best variety are the very small *mange-tout* beans,
which are no more than two inches long. The stringless variety are more common and should not be more than three
or four inches long and very green.

1 *Fagiolini al burro or vinaigrette*

Boil two pounds young french beans in plenty of salted water for ten to fifteen minutes (according to their size). Drain them, add 2 oz. butter, salt and pepper and toss

For serving cold, drain the beans once cooked, refresh quickly in cold water and drain again. Then mix with the following *Sauce Vinaigrette:*

Mix together

1 tablespoon white wine vinegar
3 tablespoons good olive oil
salt, pepper and a pinch of sugar
2 chopped spring onions.

2 *Fagiolini alla crema*

Boil two pounds of young french beans in plenty of salted water for ten minutes until still

slightly crisp. Drain and put
into a saucepan with

a pinch of salt, pepper
and sugar
a sprinkling of chopped
chives and parsley
$\frac{1}{4}$ pint cream
2 egg yolks

Heat gently together, stirring,
for five minutes but do not
boil.

3 *Fagiolini allo Zabaglione*

French beans with a fluffy egg and butter sauce

Boil two pounds of young
french beans in plenty of salted
water for ten minutes until still
slightly crisp. Drain and put in
a dish. Meanwhile prepare the
following sauce:

Put in a pan over hot water

3 egg yolks
1 tablespoon white wine
vinegar
1 teaspoon sugar
pinch of all spice
2 tablespoons cream

Beat until fluffy. Then add

Pour over the beans. Very
good with boiled ham.

4 *Fagiolini in fricassea*

French beans with a little garlic and basil

Boil two pounds of young french beans in plenty of salted water for about ten minutes. Drain and serve with the following:

In a frying pan, heat up

**2 tablespoons olive oil
1 clove garlic, squeezed
1 teaspoon chopped basil
salt and pepper**

Add the beans and toss in the sauce. Serve very hot.

Haricot beans

Fagioli

1 *Fagioli alla Romana*

Haricot beans with oil, anchovies and lemon

Use the new season's dried
beans, some commercial beans
can be old to the point that
they never soften. Soak one
pound of haricot beans
overnight in plenty of cold
water. In the morning, drain
and re-fill with cold water.
Bring slowly to the boil without
salt. Boil for about one and a
half hours or until tender,
seasoning with salt halfway
through

Meanwhile finely slice	**3 onions**
Brown them in	**3 tablespoons olive oil**

then add

6 chopped anchovies
salt, pepper and nutmeg
some of the cooking
liquor
juice of a lemon
chopped parsley

Mix with the beans and serve
very hot.

2 *Fagioli alla Fiorentina*

Haricot beans with chopped fresh herbs and velouté sauce

Soak one pound of haricot
beans in plenty of cold water,
over-night. Drain, refill with
cold water, and bring slowly to
the boil without salt. Cook for
about one and a half hours
until tender, seasoning halfway
through with salt. Meanwhile
make the following *Velouté*
sauce:

Melt in a saucepan   **1½ oz. butter**
add   **1½ oz. flour**

Cook for a few minutes

Then add   **1½ pints chicken broth**

Bring to the boil and cook for a few minutes. Remove the pan from the fire and add

juice of a lemon
3 egg yolks
1 tablespoon mixed herbs

Mix the sauce with the drained beans and serve with boiled chicken.

3 *Fagioli alla polenta*

Purée of haricot beans with butter and cream

Soak one pound of haricot beans in plenty of cold water, over-night. Drain and re-fill with cold water. Bring slowly to the boil without salt and cook for about one and a half hours until tender, adding salt half-way through. Drain and pass them through a sieve or Mouli. Then add:

4 oz. butter
¼ pint cream
salt, pepper and nutmeg

Cover with lid or paper and put in the oven for ten minutes.

4 *Crocchette di fagioli*

Croquettes of haricot beans

Make a purée of haricot beans
(as in the last recipe) and put it
in a saucepan with

1 egg
4 oz. butter
1 tablespoon white wine
vinegar
chopped balm mint
salt and pepper

Mix well and allow to cool.
Roll up into balls or little
sausages, dip them in egg and
breadcrumbs and fry them in a
frying pan in a little butter and
oil.

Jerusalem Artichokes

Carciofi di Giudea

Jerusalem artichokes are a tall leafy plant with very irregular bulbous roots. They are difficult to peel without wasting a good deal of the artichoke, it is thus easier to cook them first and peel them when they have cooled a little. Their flavour is slightly sweet and they become almost opaque when cooked.

1 Purée di carciofi di Giudea

Purée of Jerusalem artichokes

In a saucepan put

2 oz. butter
1 sliced onion
2 lb. washed chopped
artichokes
2 sticks celery
2 bay leaves
salt and pepper

Cover with a lid and stew gently on the stove for twenty minutes. Pass through a Mouli. Mix with a little thin cream to

make a purée or with about 1
pint milk to make a soup.

2 *Carciofi di Giudea alla Parmigiana*

Peel two pounds of Jerusalem
artichokes and boil them in salt
water for about twenty
minutes. Drain and cut into
fairly thick slices

Meanwhile prepare a white
sauce:

Make a roux with

$\frac{3}{4}$ oz. butter
$\frac{3}{4}$ oz. flour

Heat in a saucepan

$\frac{1}{2}$ pint milk with
$\frac{1}{2}$ peeled onion
a pinch or small bunch of
mixed herbs

Mix the milk into the roux and
when it thickens and boils,
reduce the heat and add

4 oz. grated cheese
(Parmesan, Emmenthal
or Cheddar)

Stir the cheese in, add a little
cream if the sauce is too thick
and mix into the sliced
artichokes. Sprinkle with
grated Parmesan cheese and
bake in a hot oven for fifteen
minutes.

Leeks

Porri

1   *Porri alla casalinga*

Cut off most of the green part
and the root of two and a half
pounds of leeks. Slit them, not
all the way through, from the
root up and wash thoroughly.
Put into boiling salted water
for five minutes. Drain and
refresh in cold water

Smear a shallow baking dish
with dripping, arrange the
leeks in it; add

**little pieces of dripping
a sprinkling of sugar
salt and crushed pepper
a pinch of mixed herbs**

Then barely cover with
and braise in a moderate oven
for thirty to forty minutes.

stock

2 *Porri alla crema*

Prepare six good-sized leeks
and wash them well (cut off
most of the green, the roots
and slit them half-way
through). Blanch them in
boiling salted water for ten
minutes and drain them.

Cut each leek into four,
length-ways, and arrange them
in the bottom of a buttered,
shallow oven-dish

Sprinkle with

and pour over

**coarsely ground pepper-
corns
salt
$\frac{1}{2}$ pint cream (thin)**

Bake in a moderate oven for
twenty minutes to half an hour.
Sprinkle with parsley.

3 *Porri alla Greca*

Prepare six good-sized leeks
and wash them well (cut off
most of the green, the roots
and slit them half-way
through). Cut them into four,

lengthways, and put in a large
frying-pan or oven-dish with

$\frac{1}{2}$ cup olive oil
2 oz. coriander seeds
1 cup white wine
1 cup water
salt and pepper
3 bay leaves

Bring to the boil on top of the
stove and cook without a lid,
stirring carefully until the leeks
are cooked and the juice is
reduced. Serve hot or cold.

Lentils

❧

Lenticchie

Lentils need not be soaked before being cooked but a few hours in cold water often helps, for the longer the lentils have been stored, the more dehydrated they can become.

1 *Lenticchie alla corona*

Lentils cooked with pork knuckles and anchovies

In a pan, put

**1 lb. lentils
2 knuckles pork
2 onions sliced
1 carrot sliced
6 peppercorns
2 bay leaves
2 pints stock**

Bring to the boil, skim and simmer gently until the pork and lentils are cooked (about one and a half hours). If the lentils have absorbed all the

liquid, add more as they cook.
Finally, mince or chop finely
add a pinch of

**6 anchovies
mixed herbs**

Stir these into the lentils and
serve very hot, having cut the
knuckle meat from the bone.

2 *Lenticchie alla Provenzale*

Soak one pound of lentils in
cold water for a few hours. Put
them in a pan with

**1 onion
1 carrot
salt
water**

Cover well with
and bring to the boil. Simmer
until quite soft (one and a half
to two hours). Drain them and
pass through a sieve (or Mouli)

Reheat and add
and

**2 oz. butter
4 oz. cream**

Serve with hot boiled bacon or
saddle of hare.

3   *Lenticchie alla Romagnola*

Cook one pound of lentils with

**twelve peeled tomatoes
(or 1 tin of tomatoes)
½ cup olive oil
salt and pepper
2 onions chopped very
fine
2 chopped cloves garlic**

Just cover with water and
bring to the boil. Simmer,
stirring constantly and adding
water when the lentils become
too dry

Serve with roast lamb.

Lettuce

∽

Lattuga

1 *Lettuce Salads*

Wash two lettuces using the tender leaves; leave in cold water until wanted and then shake dry. Here are three dressings which go well with lettuce—but these are only three out of many.

Lettuce Dressing 1

Chop, quite finely	**2 hard boiled egg yolks**
beat in	**1 tablespoon good olive oil**
	salt and pepper
add	**1 teaspoon mustard**
	2 tablespoons wine vinegar
	3 tablespoons olive oil

Stir well together and mix into the salad.

Lettuce Dressing 2

This is best with Cos lettuce

Mix together

salt and pepper
good pinch sugar
1 dessertspoon finely
chopped capers
2 tablespoons tarragon
vinegar
4 tablespoons good olive
oil

Cut one good Cos lettuce
across into three. Wash and
shake dry

Put in a bowl with

twelve or more
Nasturtium flowers

Mix in the dressing.

Lettuce Dressing 3

Wash and dry the lettuce

Mix together

half a clove garlic finely
crushed
salt and coarsely pounded
pepper

Pour over the lettuce

a dessertspoon chopped
chives

And mix

2 tablespoons white wine
vinegar
4 tablespoons olive oil.

2 *Lattughe farcite*

Wash six lettuces keeping them whole. Plunge them in boiling salted water until the water reboils. Drain, refresh under cold water and squeeze dry.

Carefully open out the lettuces and put a tablespoon, in each, of the following stuffing:

**6 oz. minced cooked chicken or meat
2 oz. fresh breadcrumbs
2 oz. minced chicken livers
1 egg
salt, pepper and nutmeg
pinch of mixed herbs**

Lay the lettuces in a buttered, shallow oven-dish (just large enough) and add

**1 glass marsala
2 oz. butter in pieces**

Cover with a lid and bake for twenty minutes in a moderate oven.

3 *Fritto di Lattughe*

Wash twelve small lettuces, keeping them whole. Plunge them in boiling, salted water until the water reboils. Drain, refresh under cold water and squeeze them dry

Then dip them in the following batter and deep fry, until the root is tender

Make a well with the flour, add the other ingredients and gradually mix in the flour, to a smooth cream

2 heaped tablespoons flour
1 tablespoon olive oil
1 egg yolk
2 tablespoons water
salt and pepper

Serve, perhaps, with roast chicken.

Mushrooms

Funghi

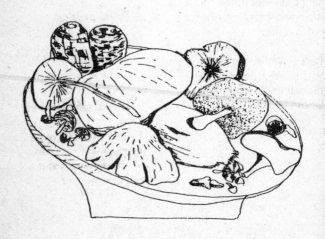

Here is a list of some of the mushrooms easily found in the Tuscan hills or bought in the markets. The cépes (*porcini*) are the most sought after and are often sliced and dried for use during the year.

Pratajnoli   (Cultivated or field mushroom)
Porcini   (Boletus edulis)
Prugnuoli   (Agaricus Georgii)
Dormienti   (Hygrophorus marzuolus)
Ovoli   (Amanita caesarea)

1 *Funghi alla crema*

Mushrooms and tarragon cream

Stew, over a good fire with	**2 lb. small mushrooms** **2 sprigs chopped tarragon** **4 oz. butter**
When the liquid has evaporated add	**salt and pepper**
Colour the mushrooms slightly, then add—still with full fire—	**½ pint thin cream**

Let it bubble until it has thickened a little, serve into little individual dishes and sprinkle with chopped parsley.

2 *Funghi alla casalinga*

Mushrooms in butter with anchovy, mint and lemon juice

Fry, in a deep frying-pan	**2 lb. mushrooms** **4 oz. butter** **1 tablespoon olive oil**

After five minutes, add	**salt and coarsely ground pepper** **4 chopped anchovies** **2 sprigs chopped mint**
Mix together and then squeeze over	**juice of 1½ lemons**

Fry for a moment longer, sprinkle with parsley and serve.

3   *Funghi alla Francese*

Mushrooms marinated in oil and herbs, and fried

In a casserole, put	**2 lb. mushrooms**
Pickle them with	**salt and pepper** **2 bay leaves chopped** **¼ pint good olive oil** **small bunch fresh chopped mixed herbs**

for one hour

Then put the casserole over a fierce fire and cook the mushrooms for ten minutes. Serve with a slice of hot ham.

4   *Funghi al pomodoro*

Mushrooms cooked with garlic and tomatoes

In a thick frying-pan, fry in	**2 lb. mushrooms** **4 tablespoons olive oil**
After five minutes add	**salt and pepper** **2 cloves chopped garlic** **8 tomatoes peeled,** **pipped and chopped**

Cook a few minutes more and sprinkle with chopped parsley.

5   *Funghi all'intingolo*

Mushrooms cooked with onions, parsley and white wine

In a thick frying-pan, fry in with	**2 lb. mushrooms** **4 oz. butter** **2 sliced onions**
Cook for eight minutes, then add	**1 glass white wine** **salt and pepper** **plenty of chopped** **parsley.**

6 Funghi alla pagnotta

This is a good way of cooking cépes or any edible funghi.

Cook the cépes as in the previous recipe and meanwhile, cut the top off a small, round loaf, scoop out the bread and fill with the mushrooms. Replace the top slice.

Put the loaf in a roasting tray on a bed of slices of streaky bacon and bake in a hot oven for fifteen minutes, basting once or twice.

7 Insalata di funghi

Slice
marinate them in

1 lb. mushrooms
olive oil
salt and pepper
chopped parsley
3 chopped anchovies
juice of a lemon

Serve after half an hour.

Onions

Cipolle

1   *Cipolle al forno*

Choose six medium-sized
onions, and without peeling
them, push a sprig of fresh
basil, marjoram or thyme into
the middle with the point of a
small knife. Wrap each one in
foil and bake in a moderate
oven until soft. Remove the
foil and the outer skin and
serve with a little melted butter
over and a sprinkling of
parsley.

2 *Cipolle farcite*

Baked, stuffed onions

Bake six large onions in metal
foil and when soft remove the
foil and outer skin. Scoop out
the centre of the onions which
are to be chopped with the
following ingredients:

**4 oz. ham (or remains of
joint)
2 oz. breadcrumbs
1 oz. melted butter
2 tablespoons cream
salt, pepper and chopped
marjoram**

Mix the stuffing well, fill the
onions, place in a baking dish
and sprinkle with grated
Parmesan and little pieces of
butter. Bake for a further
fifteen minutes in a hot oven.

3 *Cipolle fritte*

Peel and slice into rings   **4 medium onions**

Separate them into a bowl,
sprinkle milk over and leave
them for half an hour.

Drain them well and dip them
in seasoned flour. Deep fry for
three or four minutes. Drain
well and sprinkle with salt and
pepper.

4 *Cipolle glassate*

Glazed onions

Soak in cold water for a few minutes	1½ lb. small pickling onions
Peel them and put them in a frying-pan with	2 oz. butter
Toss them over a medium fire for ten minutes then add	1½ oz. sugar salt and pepper
Continue cooking without a lid with until the onions are cooked and the liquid syrupy.	½ glass port or sherry 1 glass of water

Parsnips

~

Pastinace

1   *Pastinace al burro*

Peel six young parsnips into a
basin of cold water. Cut them
in half and then into long thin
batons

Put them in a deep frying-pan
with

**3 oz. butter
juice of a lemon
salt and pepper
1 cup water
or stock**

Bring to the boil and cook,
uncovered, until the liquid is
reduced and the parsnips are
cooked (add more liquid if the
parsnips are not quite cooked).

2 *Pastinace al forno*

Parboil six peeled parsnips for
five minutes. Cut them into
batons and put them in a frying
pan with dripping. Roast them
in the oven (they can be put in
with a joint). When the
parsnips are cooked, remove
most of the fat and add a
tablespoon of flour and brown
on the fire. Add a cup of stock,
bubble for a few minutes.
Sprinkle with plenty of
Parmesan and brown for ten
minutes in the oven.

3 *Pastinace fritte*

Cut six peeled parsnips into
batons and boil them in salted
water until tender. Drain them,
sprinkle with salt and pepper,
then dip them in melted butter,
and then in a mixture of half
flour, half sugar

Heat two cups of dripping in a
deep frying pan, put in the
parsnips until they are
browned on both sides.

Peas

⌾

Piselli

It is sad that small garden peas are nowadays very difficult to find in the shops. Usually it is the pale dry pods of the field peas, whose sweetness has become starchy, that are offered. Perhaps the good quality peas are all under contract to the big freezing companies. Home-grown peas, whether the sweet garden pea or the *petit pois* variety are always the best. Most of these recipes, however, can easily be adapted by using frozen *petit pois* and adding other ingredients while the peas are still frozen.

1 *Piselli al burro*

Put a two pint jugful of shelled peas in a saucepan with

**a cup of water
4 oz. butter
salt and pepper
dessertspoon sugar
and some parsley or mint**

Place on a hot fire, when boiling remove the lid and stir

from time to time until cooked.
Remove the parsley or mint.

2 *Piselli all'antica*

Cook the peas as in the
previous recipe using a lettuce
instead of parsley or mint.
Remove the lettuce when the
peas are cooked and shake in

4 oz. thick cream

3 *Piselli alla Borghese*

Shell enough peas to fill a two
pint jug and meanwhile cook
gently
and

**1 finely chopped onion
2 chopped slices of ham
in 2 oz. butter**

Add the peas, a bunch of
herbs, salt and pepper and

2 cups of good stock

Boil fiercely until cooked and
the liquid has reduced.

4 *Piselli alla Francese*

Put a two pint jugful of shelled
peas in a saucepan with

2 chopped lettuces
1 chopped onion
stewed in butter
salt and pepper
2 cups good stock

Cook over a good heat, stirring
from time to time.

5 *Piselli nel guscio*

Peas in their pods

Remove the stalks from two
pounds of very young peas and
cook them in their pods in
plenty of boiling salted water
for nearly half an hour, drain
and serve with melted butter.

6 *Sformato di pisseli*

Pease-pudding

Boil two pints of large shelled
peas in
with
and a

1 pint strong stock
salt and pepper
pinch of allspice

When cooked pass the peas
through a fine sieve and return
to a low flame, adding

2 oz. butter
1 tablespoon flour
3 yolks of eggs
2 crushed macaroons

Heat through stirring well,
remove from the fire and cool
slightly while you beat

three egg whites

Fold them in and put the
mixture in a buttered soufflé
dish. Cook in a container of
hot water in a moderate oven
for half an hour.

Polenta

~

Maize Flour

Maize flour is not much used now, even in Italy, where Northerners are sometimes called *polentoni* by the Southerners. The most successful use for maize flour is in making bread when it would be mixed with wheat flour; two-thirds maize flour to one-third wheat flour. It is a bread that goes well with a meal, particularly a simple meal of salami and cheese.

1. *Polenta alla Parmigiana*

Stir, a little at a time, into
1 pint boiling salted water
1 lb. Indian cornflour

Boil until smooth, then turn out into an oiled tray, spreading out the mixture until it is half an inch thick

When cool cut it into thick pieces and pile in layers in a baking dish interspersed,

liberally, with melted butter
and grated Parmesan, finishing
with butter and Parmesan.
Bake in a medium oven for
forty minutes.

2 *Polenta on salcicce*

Polenta with garlic sausage or zampone

Make the polenta as in the last
recipe and cool on a tray.
While it is cooking, boil some
garlic sausage—or the rich
Italian *zampone,* for half an
hour

Skin and dice the sausage, mix
it with some tomato purée and
a little stock. Pile alternate
layers of polenta and sausage
in a baking dish with grated
Parmesan and pieces of butter
between each layer. Sprinkle
finally with Parmesan and
butter and bake in the oven for
half an hour

Serve very hot with a crisp
salad with a slightly sweetened
dressing.

Potatoes

Patate

1   Patate alla Borghese

Potatoes with butter and lemon

Boil two pounds of potatoes in
their skins (or two pounds of
new potatoes scraped). Drain
and peel them and cut in thick
slices into a shallow oven-
proof dish

Add

**4 oz. butter
chopped parsley
salt and pepper**

Simmer with a lid and add

the juice of 2 lemons

Serve hot.

2 *Patate alla campagnuola*

Sliced potatoes with nutmeg and cream

Boil two pounds of potatoes in
their skins, drain, peel and
slice them thin

Heat them in a thick frying pan
with

4 oz. butter
salt and pepper
nutmeg

Colour slightly, add

¼ pint cream

Shake thoroughly and serve
hot.

3 *Patate in casseruola*

A ring of mashed potatoes with a centre of tomato pulp

Peel and chop
put in a pan with
and

8 good-sized ripe
tomatoes
juice of ½ an onion
2 tablespoons olive oil
salt and pepper

Cook slowly while you prepare
the potatoes

Potatoes/*Patate*

Mix in a saucepan, over a low
fire

1 lb. mashed potato
4 egg yolks
¼ pint cream
2 oz. butter

Stir frequently until the
potatoes form a paste then
season with
and arrange in spoonfuls round
a dish

salt and pepper

Pour the tomato into the centre
of the ring and sprinkle with
grated Parmesan.

4 *Patate alla crema*

Boil twelve potatoes in their
skins. Drain, peel and chop them

In a pan, put

4 oz. butter
½ onion chopped
chopped parsley
chopped mint
salt and pepper

Stew with a lid on until the
onion is cooked. Then remove
the lid, mix in the potatoes and
a cup of single cream

Shake well until the mixture
boils. Sprinkle with parsley
and serve.

5   *Crocchette di patate*

Boil eight potatoes. Drain well
and leave the pan on the side
of the stove for a minute to dry
out the potatoes

Put them through a sieve or
Mouli and put the purée in the
saucepan with:

2 egg yolks
a little grated onion
juice of a lemon
chopped parsley
2 oz. butter
2 tablespoons of cream
a pinch of cinnamon and
grated nutmeg
salt and pepper

Mix the purée with these
ingredients thoroughly with a
wooden spoon on a low fire
until the mixture stiffens.
When cool, roll into little
sausages on a floured board.
Egg and breadcrumb and fry in
hot fat until golden.

6   *Patate al forno*

Bake six large potatoes. When
cooked, cut them in two and
remove the insides with a

spoon. Mash the scooped out
potato with a fork and add

4 oz. butter
½ pint hot milk
salt and pepper
6 crushed juniper berries

Mix well together and add the
beaten

whites of 2 eggs

Fill the skins with the paste
and fork over the top

Cook in a hot oven until crisp
and golden.

7 *Gnocchi di patate*

Boil eight potatoes. Drain well
and leave to dry for a minute
on the side of the stove. Pass
through a sieve or Mouli,
return the purée to the
saucepan and add:

2 oz. grated Parmesan
2 oz. flour
3 eggs
salt, pepper and nutmeg

Mix well and cool

Make into little rolls on a
floured board. Put them—a
dozen at a time into boiling
salted water (do not boil
fiercely) for a few minutes

until they rise and are firm.
Place on a dish in a cool oven
until they are all done, then
pour over melted butter and
sprinkle with grated Parmesan.

8 *Patate all'Italiana*

Wash and peel off a strip round
eight potatoes. Boil in salted
water for twenty minutes until
cooked. Drain them well and
sieve them. Put them back in
the pan with

2 oz. butter
4 slices crustless bread
soaked in milk
$\frac{1}{2}$ cup milk
3 egg yolks
salt, pepper and nutmeg

Mix well together and add

3 beaten egg whites

Pile high in a baking dish,
sprinkle with melted butter and
grated Parmesan and bake
until golden for fifteen to
twenty minutes.

9 *Budino di patate con funghi*

Boil eight potatoes,
meanwhile, quarter and fry in
butter
add

**1 lb. open mushrooms
salt and crushed
peppercorns
2 tablespoons cream**

Shake the pan and reserve
until the potato purée is made

Drain and sieve the potatoes.
Add

**2 oz. butter
$\frac{1}{2}$ cup cream
3 egg yolks
salt and good pinch
pepper**

Butter a soufflé dish and put
the purée in the bottom and
sides leaving a well in the
middle and some purée to put
on top. Put the cooked
mushrooms in the middle and
seal with the rest of the purée.
Cook for twenty minutes in the
oven and turn out onto a dish
(but leave in the dish if the
potato has stuck to it).

Note. This potato purée can
have a variety of
fillings—leeks, spinach, small
broad beans all mixed with a
little cream.

10 *Patate arrostite*

Scrape three pounds of new
equal-sized round new
potatoes

Heat
and
in a large deep frying-pan and
add

4 oz. butter
2 tablespoons olive oil

the potatoes, salt and
pepper

Cover with a lid, place on a
fairly low fire and shake
frequently. They will take a
good half hour and should
have a good brown crust.

11 *Patate in stufato*

Cut six large peeled potatoes
into approximately quarter-
inch cubes. Put them in a
baking dish just covered with
milk. Sprinkle with 2 oz.
butter, cover and bring to the
boil then put in a hot oven
until tender (still with the lid
on).

12 *Patate Tartufate*

Potatoes cooked with truffles and Parmesan

Slice four large potatoes fairly
thin and wash them in cold
water. Lay them in a buttered
baking dish with layers of
potato, sliced Piedmontese
white truffles (if you can get
them) and grated Parmesan
cheese. Finish with grated
Parmesan, sprinkle with butter
and lemon juice and moisten
with good chicken broth (about
half way up the baking dish).
Bake in a fairly hot oven until
tender (about forty minutes).

13 *Insalata di patate con vino e acciughe*

Potato Salad with wine and anchovies

Mix six finely sliced cooked
potatoes with

1 bunch spring onions,
chopped
1 glass red wine
salt and crushed pepper
1 cup olive oil
$\frac{1}{2}$ tablespoon wine vinegar
chopped chervil and
parsley
twelve roughly chopped
anchovies

Mix together and leave to
marinate before serving.

14 *Insalata di patate*

Potato salad

Slice six cooked potatoes.
Slice 3 hard boiled eggs and
mince 6 oz. tunny fish. Place
alternate layers of potato, egg
and minced tunny fish. Pour
over a *Vinaigrette* in which
there is chopped fresh fennel.

Pumpkin

Zucca

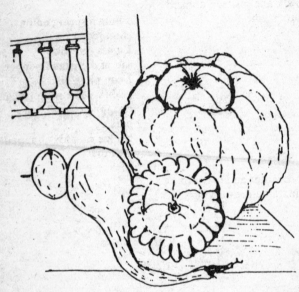

1   *Zucche ripiene*

Small pumpkins filled with tunny fish and spice, served
with tomato sauce

Cut in half either three small
American squashes (the size of

your fist) or six large courgettes—about six inches long

Scoop out the insides with a dessertspoon, throwing away the seeds but preserving the pulp

Mix the pulp with

3 egg yolks
an 8-oz. tin of tunny fish with
the oil
1 tablespoon grated Parmesan
pinch of allspice and pepper
small pinch salt

Fill the half pumpkin shells with the mixture. Sprinkle with more grated Parmesan and bake in a moderate oven with a lid

Serve with a tomato *coulis*, made simply by sweating

½ finely chopped onion in olive oil

When cooked, pour in add

1 tin Italian tomatoes
salt and pepper

Stew for twenty minutes and serve.

2 *Zucche fritte*

Strips of pumpkin or marrow fried in olive oil

Peel, halve and seed six
courgettes (about six inches
long) or one small pumpkin
(smaller than a football). Cut
the flesh into strips, the size of
chips and leave them in a sieve
sprinkled with salt for a couple
of hours (to get rid of excess
moisture)

Heat olive oil (or frying oil) in
deep pan. Dip the strips in
seasoned flour and fry until
cooked and light brown

Drain well and serve at once,
with a squeeze of lemon.

3   *Zucche alla Fiorentina*

Boil three small American
squashes in salted water. When
soft drain, cut in half and
remove the seeds

In the middle put

**cream
a small knob of butter
salt, pepper and nutmeg
squeeze of lemon**

Bake in a hot oven for ten
minutes

Sprinkle with chopped chives
and serve.

Sorrel Purée

❧

Puré di acetosa

The most practical way of using sorrel is to make it into a buttery purée which will keep in a glass jar in the refrigerator. This can be used for a soup, a fish sauce, an omelette, mixed in with some young cooked peas, or with chopped cooked potatoes and cream.

Wash the sorrel carefully and put it into a pan with a little boiling water, season lightly and cover. Uncover and stir now and again until the sorrel is soft and a brownish colour (only three to four minutes). Drain and mix with melted butter. Keep in the refrigerator until needed.

Spinach

Spinaci

1 *Spinaci al burro*

Remove the stalks and wash
two pounds of spinach in a
sink full of cold water. Drain
the spinach and shred it.

In an earthenware pot put 2
oz. butter and when this has
melted add the spinach, salt
and pepper and a lid. Stir
constantly until the spinach is
cooked. If the spinach appears
too wet when almost cooked,
remove the lid and finish
cooking until the juices have
evaporated.

2 *Spinaci alla crema*

Remove the stalks and wash
two pounds of spinach in a
sink full of cold water. Drain
and chop it.

Melt 2 oz. butter in an
earthenware pot, and add the
spinach, salt and pepper.
Cover with a lid removing it to
stir the spinach constantly.
When the spinach is cooked
remove it from the pan and let
the juices bubble.

Stir in 1 dessertspoon ($\frac{1}{2}$ oz.)
flour and $\frac{1}{4}$ pint cream, stir
until it bubbles and thickens,
add the spinach and a little
grated nutmeg and 3 hard
boiled eggs roughly chopped.
Reheat thoroughly and serve.

3 *Crocchette di spinaci*

Remove the stalks and wash
two pounds of spinach in a
sink full of cold water. Drain
well, chop and put in an

earthenware pot with salt and pepper. Stir frequently and cover with a lid. When cooked drain it and press dry. Chop it again and replace it in the earthenware pot with

4 oz. butter
a small bunch of marjoram, chopped
1 teaspoon of sugar
a little grated zest of lemon

and

Mix well over the fire and put in

¼ pint milk

When it boils add

2 beaten-up eggs

Remove from the fire and stir until the egg thickens. Allow to cool. Then roll into small sausages

Meanwhile make the batter:

Mix the oil and wine or water into

2 oz. flour
1 tablespoon olive oil
½ glass white wine (or water)
salt

Roll the croquette in this batter and deep fry

Serve with sections of lemon.

Spinach/*Spinaci*

4   *Ravioli alla Fiorentina*

Remove the stalks and wash
two pounds of spinach. Drain
and cook in boiling salted
water. When the water reboils,
drain the spinach. Run cold
water over it and press it very
dry with the hands. Chop finely
and put in a saucepan with

1 oz. flour
2 oz. butter
8 oz. fresh curd cheese
(Ricotta)
3 egg yolks
salt, pepper and nutmeg
2 oz. grated Parmesan

Stir briskly for a minute or two
and allow to cool. When cold
roll into small pointed sausages
(an inch long) flour them and
lower them into boiling salted
water. Simmer and as they rise
remove them from the fire.
Pour over melted butter,
sprinkle with grated Parmesan
and serve.

5 *Spinaci in riccioli*

Remove the stalks and wash one pound of spinach, boil in salted water for a few minutes, drain well. Rub it through a sieve (alternatively use frozen chopped spinach). Beat up 2 eggs with salt and pepper and mix in the spinach

Pour a little olive oil into an omelette- or pancake-pan, heat thoroughly and pour in a little of the mixture as for making a pancake, i.e. as thin as possible. Turn it over, take it out and repeat until all the mixture is used, stacking the pancakes on top of one another

Shred the pancakes into fingers and pour a purée of tomatoes (simply tomatoes and seasoning sweated in oil with a lid on and then passed through a sieve) over them and sprinkle with Parmesan. Brown in a hot oven

Good with smoked sausages or the pancakes shredded into consommé.

6 *Sformato di spinaci*

Spinach soufflé

Wash, cook and sieve	**2 lb. spinach**
heat in a saucepan	**1½ oz. butter**
add and cook	**1½ oz. flour**
add and bring to the boil	**¼ pint thin cream**
season with	**salt, pepper and nutmeg**
mix in without boiling	**2 egg yolks**
when cool, whisk and fold in	**3 egg whites**

Half fill individual soufflé dishes. Sprinkle well with Parmesan and bake in a moderate to hot oven for ten to fifteen minutes depending on the size of the dish.

Serve, needless to say, at once.

Note. If this is cooked for a party, prepare the soufflé base ahead with all but the egg whites in it. The base should be warm but not hot or cold. Whip and fold in the egg whites so that the soufflé will be cooked when you wish to eat.

7   *Sformato di spinaci con funghi*

Either make a purée of spinach (as in *spinace in Riccioli*) or heat two half-pound packets of frozen spinach purée in

2 oz. butter

Cook until fairly dry. Add the juice of

$\frac{1}{2}$ **a lemon**

Leave to cool. Beat up with

3 egg yolks
one whole egg

Butter a mould—preferably a ring mould but if not, a soufflé dish. Add the spinach to the egg and the mixture to the mould. Cook *au bain marie* for an hour in a moderate oven and when set, turn out and pour mushrooms fried with a little garlic and finished with tomatoes and seasoning into the middle.

Tomato

Pomodori

1 Conserva di pomodori

Tomato conserve

Wash as many ripe or nearly
ripe (not over ripe) tomatoes as
you wish. Put them in a deep
saucepan, sprinkle with salt
and pepper and sugar, put on a
lid and cook slowly, stirring
from time to time until the
tomatoes are a pulp

Pass the pulp through a Mouli
or sieve and preserve in jars or
keep it in a refrigerator with
olive oil on top or, in these
days of large deep freezes,
pour the cold purée into
polythene bags and freeze until
needed

This purée is a basic ingredient
to much of Italian cooking. It
is used in soups, risottos,
sauces and many meat dishes.

2   *Pomodori alla griglia alla senape*

Grilled tomatoes with a mustard dressing

Halve six large ripe tomatoes
without skinning them and put
them to grill cut side up with
salt, pepper and a brushing of
olive oil

While they are grilling baste
with a dressing of

**1 tablespoon olive oil
juice of $\frac{1}{2}$ a lemon
small teaspoon sugar
small teaspoon French
mustard
little salt and pepper**

Place the tomatoes in a hot
dish with the dressing. Sprinkle
with parsley.

3   *Pomodori al forno*

Cut six large ripe tomatoes in
half without skinning them.

Scoop out some of the pips and
centre with a teaspoon.
Prepare a stuffing with
sweated in

six sliced mushrooms
1 tablespoon olive oil
chopped small clove of
garlic
pinch of chopped parsley
pinch of chopped chives

Fill the tomatoes with the
stuffing and sprinkle with
Parmesan

Bake for ten to fifteen minutes.

4 *Pomodori alla panna*

Scald and peel twelve small
ripe tomatoes

Heat in an earthenware pan
sweat without colour
add

1 tablespoon olive oil
1 chopped onion
1 tablespoon chopped
fresh marjoram
$\frac{1}{2}$ oz. flour
salt and pepper
$\frac{1}{4}$ pint thin cream

Cook for a minute and add

Bring the cream to the boil,
shaking the pan occasionally.
Add the tomatoes and cook on
top or in the very hot oven for
five minutes or until the
tomatoes are cooked. Serve
sprinkled with chopped
parsley.

5   *Pomodori con uova*

Take six large tomatoes, cut
off the top and keep it aside to
make a lid. Scoop out the
middle carefully and break an
egg into each tomato. Season
with salt and pepper and a
little chopped tarragon, add a
nut of butter and replace the
tomato lid. Place the tomatoes
on a well buttered dish and
season them lightly. Bake in a
very hot oven until the eggs
are set (10–12 minutes)

The tomatoes can be served on
a round base of buttered toast
covered with a slice of ham

Other tomato stuffings:

1) left over risotto
2) chopped anchovies,
olives, and garlic and
breadcrumbs
3) chopped mushrooms
and shrimps
4) flaked cooked smoked
haddock—serve with
garlic mayonnaise

6 *Gelatina di pomodori*

Tomato jelly

Heat one pint of tomato preserve

Add	1 tablespoon finely chopped chives
	juice of a lemon to taste
	pinch of cayenne
Pour over	one ½ oz. packet of dissolved gelatine

and pour into a ring mould

Turn out when set and fill the centre with fresh prawns mixed with a little mayonnaise.

7 *Insalata di pomodori*

Tomato salads

a) Slice six tomatoes (peeled first or not, according to your wish) and dress with	1 tablespoon tarragon vinegar
	2 tablespoons good olive oil
	sprinkling of sugar and salt
	chopped chives

b) Scald and peel six tomatoes. Halve them and scoop out the seeds (keep them for a soup or stew). Fill the tomatoes with chopped hard boiled egg mixed with mayonnaise and chopped tarragon.

c) Slice the tomatoes. Chop some celery very finely and sprinkle over them. Pour over some *Vinaigrette* dressing.

d) Slice the tomatoes and make a lattice work over them with thin strips of anchovy. Roughly chop some stoned black olives and sprinkle over. Pour over a little *Vinaigrette* dressing to which has been added a little crushed garlic. Choose large tomatoes, peel them (if preferred) and slice them lengthways. Alternate the 2 slices of peeled Italian peach, overlapping well. Season with salt and pepper, sprinkle lemon juice over and a little walnut oil.

Mixed Vegetables and Salads

1 Sformato di verdura

Flan of vegetables baked vegetable cake

Use of a total of of which there should be	3 lb. mixed vegetables 1 lb. potatoes
Prepare them and cut them up fairly small. Put them in a saucepan with	2 oz. melted butter 1 cup water salt and pepper 1 bunch sweet herbs
Cover with a lid and stew gently until cooked. Then add	1 cup cream
Stir and leave to cool	
Mix in	4 yolks of eggs 4 oz. grated cheese
and fold in	4 beaten egg whites

144

Put the mixture in a buttered mould, well lined with breadcrumbs, cover with more breadcrumbs and a buttered paper and bake in a moderate oven for forty minutes.

2 *Verdure miste brasate*

Mixed braised vegetables (a winter dish)

Prepare the following vegetables, cutting the carrots, turnips and leeks into three-inch strips

$\frac{1}{4}$ lb. small onions
$\frac{1}{4}$ lb. carrots
$\frac{1}{2}$ lb. turnips
$\frac{1}{4}$ lb. leeks
$\frac{1}{2}$ lb. celery
$\frac{1}{2}$ 1 medium cabbage

Arrange the onions, carrots, turnips and leeks in a large shallow oven dish. Almost add

cover with stock
salt and pepper
pinch of mixed herbs

Braise in a moderate oven for half an hour.

Meanwhile, blanch the cabbage for five minutes in boiling salted water. Drain and cut into six pieces, each with a

little stalk; arrange the cabbage
with the other vegetables.
Cook for a further twenty
minutes.

Sprinkle with plenty of parsley.
Take care that the vegetables
are not over-cooked for the
flavour will lose freshness and
become 'gassy'.

3   *Cappon magro*

A mixture of spring vegetables, piled up into a pyramid.
Serve with a plain roast

This mixture can vary a good
deal but this list will indicate
some of the range of choice.
Use at east six of them:

small new potatoes
small onions
baby carrots
small french beans
courgettes
bulb fennel
small sliced artichokes
broad beans
asparagus
baby cauliflower
small peas
tomatoes

The only rule to follow is that
the root vegetables should be

cooked separately, starting
with cold water. The others in
boiling water.

The vegetables, when cooked
and drained are mixed together
and tossed in melted butter and
more salt and pepper.

4 Fritto misto

Mixed fried vegetables

Traditionally, this is a dish of
fried vegetables with fried
calves brains and chicken
rissoles. The following recipe,
however, omits the meat.

Prepare the following
vegetables:

Pare, cut into slices and keep
in cold water   **6 young artichokes**

Top and tail and cut into long $\frac{1}{4}$
in. strips   **4 small courgettes**

Quarter and take out the seeds
of   **3 red peppers**

Blanch, for five minutes and
separate into flowers   **1 small cauliflower**

Finally fill, with the following stuffing	**twelve courgettes flowers**
Clean, cook and squeeze dry mix in	**1 lb. spinach** **3 demi-sel cheeses** **1 egg** **salt, pepper and nutmeg**

Fry all these vegetables, in stages, in deep fat, first dipping them in the following batter:

Put in a bowl and make a well with	**4 oz. flour** **salt and pepper**
In the well, put	**2 egg yolks** **3 tablespoons olive oil**
Start mixing in the flour and gradually add until it is smooth and like thick cream	**½ pint water**
Finally, add	**2 beaten egg whites**

Mixed Salads

∽

Insalate miste

1 *alla Cardinale*

Wash a lettuce and a bunch of
watercress

Cut into strips	**3 small beetroot**
Quarter	**3 hard boiled eggs**
Wash	**twelve radishes**
Slice	**½ cucumber**

Arrange them all on a shallow
dish and serve with a creamy
mayonnaise:

Put, in a bowl	**2 egg yolks**
Very gradually add and	**¼ pint olive oil** **1 dessertspoon white wine vinegar**

| Add | salt and pepper |
| and | 2 tablespoons cream |

2 *all' Italiana*

| Cook | 1 lb. new potatoes in their skins |
| and | ½ lb. baby carrots |

Peel the potatoes. When cold, cut the potatoes and carrots into slices.

| Then cut | 2 washed leeks |

into 2 in. lengths, then in half and then shred very finely

Mix the vegetables together with the following Sauce Lombarda:

In a bowl, put very gradually add	2 egg yolks
	¼ pint olive oil
	salt and pepper
	1 dessertspoon lemon juice
	1 dessertspoon tomato purée
	1 dessertspoon chopped fresh herbs

3 *alla Macedone*

Mix together

$\frac{1}{2}$ lb. cooked french beans
$\frac{1}{2}$ lb. cooked young peas
$\frac{1}{4}$ lb. soaked and cooked
haricot beans

Dress with the following
Vinaigrette — the olive oil
should be
the finest:

2 tablespoons wine
vinegar
salt and pepper
1 tablespoon chopped
chives
4 tablespoons olive oil

4 *alla pollastra*

Arrange on a dish the
following:

2 sliced peppers
6 tomatoes quartered
the remains of a cold
chicken
1 small Cos lettuce
shredded
24 stoned olives

Make a *Vinaigrette* sauce with
salt, pepper, sugar, vinegar and
olive oil and add a little cream.
Pour over the salad.

5 *alla Russa*

Mixed salad with prawns, capers, anchovies and mock
caviare dressing

Cut up and mix together	
cooked	**asparagus**
	french beans
	peas
	young carrots
add	**some capers**
	anchovies
	prawns
Pour over a sauce made with	**salt and cayenne pepper**
	1 teaspoon mustard
	½ grated onion
	small jar Danish 'caviare'
	3 tablespoons vinegar
	6 tablespoons olive oil

Rice

Riso

Cooking Rice

Wash the rice and pour it into plenty of boiling salted water.
Stir the rice until the water reboils, and continue boiling for
about a quarter of an hour until the rice is just soft between
the teeth. Drain it in a colander and rinse briefly under hot
water, serve or put in a buttered casserole, cover with a lid
and keep hot—but not too hot.

The basic difference between a pilaf and a risotto is firstly the amount of liquid in which the fried rice is cooked. Pilaf should be dry and have the same quantity of liquid as of rice, a risotto should be moist and needs half as much liquid again as a pilaf. Secondly, whereas a pilaf is a plain, flavoured rice dish (say with saffron or herbs) usually served as an accompaniment; a risotto has a high proportion of additional ingredients, making it a dish in itself. The commonest mistake with a risotto is to have too high a proportion of rice.

The rice in pilafs and risottos should be fried first in the best olive oil obtainable. Pilafs and risottos should 'repose' for a few minutes once they are cooked. The rice, during this time absorbs more moisture.

1 Pilaf

Fry, in an earthenware pot in	½ finely chopped onion 2 tablespoons good olive oil
add and fry add	8 oz. rice 1¼ pint stock or water and bouillon cube 1 bay leaf salt and pepper if necessary

Bring to the boil, cover and simmer gently on top of the stove or in a moderate oven for nearly half an hour until the rice is cooked. Remove this from the stove and leave

without a lid in a warm place
or oven for a few minutes and
serve.

2   *Riso alla Ristori*

In an earthenware casserole
put

4 oz. green bacon,
chopped
1 chopped onion
$\frac{1}{4}$ to $\frac{1}{2}$ shredded white
cabbage
a little salt, pepper and
sugar
6 slices garlic sausage,
quartered

Cover with a lid and stew for
half an hour, add

4 oz. Italian or Patna rice
$\frac{3}{4}$ pint stock
1 tablespoon chopped
parsley

Simmer gently for a further
twenty minutes and serve with
grated Parmesan.

3 *Riso al pomodoro*

In an earthenware casserole put	**2 tablespoons olive oil**
add	**1 finely chopped onion**
	1 chopped clove garlic

and stew without colouring

Add and fry	**8 oz. Italian rice**
add	**1 tablespoon chopped marjoram**
	1 pint tomato pulp (see p. 138)
	salt and pepper

Bring to the boil, simmer for about twenty minutes until the rice is almost cooked, remove from the fire and leave to rest for five minutes before serving with grated Parmesan.

4 *Risotto ai funghi secchi*

Rice with dried cèpes

In a small bowl soak in warm water	**2 oz. dried cèpes**
In an earthenware casserole heat	**2 tablespoons olive oil**

Add and fry without colouring and	1 finely chopped onion 1 good clove of garlic chopped
Add and fry	6 oz. Avorio rice
Add the soaked and chopped	cèpes pinch of thyme 1 pint stock or water and chicken bouillon cube mill ground pepper

Bring to the boil, simmer gently for twenty to twenty-five minutes. Leave to rest for five minutes and sprinkle with parsley and cheese.

5 *Risotto ai gamberi*

Risotto with prawns

In an earthenware casserole put	2 tablespoons olive oil
Add and fry without colouring and	1 finely chopped onion 1 chopped clove garlic
Then add and fry and	6 oz. Italian rice twelve good-sized Mediterranean prawns in their shells

Add	1 level dessertspoon of tomato purée
	juice of a lemon
	pinch of mixed herbs
	pinch of cayenne
	1 pint water with chicken bouillon cube

Bring to the boil, simmer in a moderate oven with a lid for nearly twenty minutes until the rice is just soft to the bite. Put the risotto to one side to 'repose', correct the seasoning and serve.

6   *Riso pilaf allo zafferano*

Saffron Pilaf

In an earthenware casserole put	2 tablespoons olive oil
Add and fry without colour	1 finely chopped onion
add	8 oz. Italian or Patna rice
and	½ coffee-spoon crushed saffron
Fry the rice and add	1 pint stock
and the	juice of one lemon

Bring to the boil, cover with a lid and simmer in the oven or

on top for about twenty
minutes until the rice is really
cooked. Take off the heat and
leave it to stand for five
minutes.

7   *Risotto alla Poggio Gherardo*

Risotto with marsala and chicken livers

In an earthenware casserole heat	**2 tablespoons olive oil**
Add and fry	**1 chopped onion** **6 oz. rice**
Then add	**1 port glass marsala**
Let it bubble almost dry and add and	**1 pint chicken stock** **small pinch of mixed herbs** **good pinch crushed pepper**
Then add	**4 chopped chicken livers (roughly 4 oz.)**

Simmer for twenty minutes.
Let the rice rest for five
minutes and serve with grated
Parmesan.

8 *Risotto alla Milanese*

In an earthenware casserole heat and	2 tablespoons olive oil 1 oz. butter
In this fry golden	1 chopped onion
Add	6 oz. sliced mushrooms a large pinch crushed saffron (1 chopped truffle)
Stir in and fry	6 oz. Avorio rice
Add and	1 pint chicken stock 1½ oz. grated Parmesan

Simmer for eighteen minutes.
Let it rest and serve with
grated Parmesan.

9 *Crocchette di riso a spinaci*

For using cooked rice

Mix together

**8 tablespoons cooked rice
1 lb. cooked spinach
squeezed dry and
chopped
2 eggs
ground nutmeg
salt and pepper
1 oz. grated Parmesan
grated rind of one lemon**

Bind, if too soft, with a little
flour. Then with floured hands
roll into sausages on a floured
board and dip in beaten egg
and breadcrumbs and fry
golden.

Macaroni

&

Pasta Asciutta

Making *pasta* is not difficult nor does it take too long but space in the form of a good-sized kitchen table is essential for rolling out the paste as thin as paper. In Italy there always seem to be a few black clad grandmothers and aunts who have the build for kneading and the time to spare.

The commercial pasta, however, is fairly good—except for perhaps with *lasagne* and *ravioli* where the fresh pasta is noticeably better. Some fifty varieties are presented in the catalogues of pasta manufacturers; tubes, shells, rods, nuts and bolts, the whole display having the appearance of an ironmonger's advertisement.

The commercial *lasagne* needs blanching for ten to fifteen minutes, unlike the home-made which only needs five minutes in boiling salted water. The *fettucini* and macaroni to be served simply with butter and cheese or with a sauce will need a little more than fifteen minutes depending on its shape and size. When cooked, it should be *al dente*—with a slight bite to it. Someone I know, hurls a strand of spaghetti at the wall and if it sticks, it is cooked.

To make Pasta

In a basin put	**1 lb. plain flour**
Make a well and break in	**3 eggs**
Add	**1 scant teaspoon salt**

162

Break up the eggs with a
wooden spoon and gradually
incorporate the flour gradually
adding about

4 fluid oz. water

Then knead until elastic (about five minutes). Divide the
paste and roll out paper thin until just about transparent,
dusting lightly and frequently with flour. Leave to rest for
half an hour and then cut as required into oblongs for *lasagne* and *cannelloni*; small squares for ravioli or rolled and
shredded for *tagliatelle*.

1   *Fettucine alla crema*

'Ribbons' served with cheese and cream

Stick an onion with a clove
and cook it with one pound of
fettucini or *tagliatelle* in boiling
salted water for nearly twenty
minutes. When just cooked,
drain well and remove the
onion

Return to the saucepan with

2 oz. butter
4 oz. grated Emmenthal
2 oz. grated Parmesan
pinch of nutmeg
a little grated nutmeg
6 fluid oz. cream

Cook for a few minutes over a
low flame until the cheese
melts and becomes elastic.
Serve very hot.

2 *Maccheroni al forno*

Lasagne baked with mozzarella cheese

Blanch one pound of *lasagne*
in boiling salted water or stock
for fifteen minutes until just
soft. Meanwhile, slice two
mozzarella cheeses thinly
(these can be bought in Soho).
Drain the pasta when cooked
and refresh under running hot
water. In a thick baking dish
alternate the pasta with layers
of cheese, seasoned with
ground pepper, nutmeg and
grated Parmesan. Finish with
pasta, sprinkle with grated
Parmesan, breadcrumbs and a
few small nuts of butter, bake
in a hot oven until brown and
sizzling. (Beware, the
mozzarella will be extremely
elastic.)

3 *Spaghetti alla Napoletana*

A sauce of mushrooms (white truffles) tongue and tomatoes

Cook one pound of spaghetti
for nearly twenty minutes until
just soft. Drain it well and

return it to the saucepan and
pour over the following sauce:

In a small saucepan heat	**1 tablespoon olive oil**
Add and fry, without colour	**1 small chopped onion**
Add and cook	**$\frac{1}{4}$ lb. chopped mushrooms**
Then add	**1 small tin of tomatoes, crushed** **salt and pepper** **a little chopped white truffle** **2 oz. chopped tongue**

Simmer gently for five
minutes, serve very hot and
also with grated Parmesan.

4 *Spaghetti alla Quaresima*

Spaghetti with parsley, anchovies and white wine

Boil one pound of spaghetti in
salted water for about twenty
minutes until just soft. Drain
well and serve with the
following sauce:

Heat, in a small saucepan	**1 tablespoon olive oil**

In it, fry golden,	**1 large chopped onion** **1 clove chopped garlic** **8 chopped anchovies** **1 glass white wine**
Reduce the wine and add	**8 fluid oz. fish stock** **(from a turbot or cod's** **head) or water**
Season with	**a pinch of white pepper** **2 tablespoons chopped** **parsley**

Serve this sauce with the
spaghetti and a bowl of grated
Parmesan. Flaked fish,
prawns, mussels or squid can
be added to the sauce.

5 *Maccheroni alla Siciliana*

Lasagne cooked with chopped cooked veal, ham, eggs and
herbs

Blanch three-quarters of a
pound of *lasagne* for fifteen
minutes until nearly soft, drain
and refresh under hot running
water

Meanwhile chop	**1 lb. cooked veal (beef or** **lamb will do)**
and	**4 oz. ham**

Slice and chop	**4 hard-boiled eggs** **2 tablespoons marjoram,** **chives, little basil and** **chervil**

Butter a baking dish (a fairly shallow casserole). Lay pieces of *pasta* on the bottom, then meat, eggs, herbs and seasoning, more *pasta*, another layer of meat etc, and finally a layer of *pasta*

Pour in enough	**stock or water with** **chicken bouillon**

nearly to cover.

Sprinkle with grated Parmesan and a few small nuts of butter and bake in a hot oven for twenty minutes until browned.

6 Timballo ai funghi

Cooked *fettucini* coiled inside a mould filled with *fettucini* and mushroom sauce; then baked

Cook one pound of *fettucini* in boiling salted water until nearly soft. Drain and allow to cool. Butter a timbale mould or pudding basin (about seven inches in diameter)

Meanwhile prepare the
following sauce:

Melt in a frying pan	**2 oz. butter**
add	**1 chopped clove garlic**
and	**8 oz. sliced button mushrooms**

Cook until the moisture of the mushrooms has evaporated and add	**1 oz. flour**

Mix in and add	**½ pint good stock** **1 tablespoon chopped marjoram** **salt and pepper**

Simmer for ten minutes

Coil some of the cool *fettucini*
round the inside of the timbale
well packed and slightly
overlapping until the sides and
base are covered. Mix the
sauce with the remainder of
the *fettucini* and pour into the
middle of the mould. Put the
mould in a baking dish of
water, cover the mould with a
saucer and place in a moderate
oven for forty minutes

Turn out carefully on to a hot
dish and serve with grated
Parmesan and a fresh purée of
tomatoes (twelve tomatoes
squashed into a saucepan,
seasoned, covered and stewed
for ten minutes and then
passed through the Mouli).

7 *Pappardelle con lepre*

Wide noodles with hare sauce

Cook some wide strip noodles
(wider than *fettucini*) in boiling
salted water until nearly soft
(about twenty minutes), drain
and mix with the following
sauce made from legs and
shoulder of hare. (Use the
saddle of hare for roasting.)

In a thick frying pan heat	**1 tablespoon olive oil**
Add	**4 oz. streaky bacon chopped** **½ chopped onion** **1 clove garlic chopped** **1 chopped piece of celery**
When brown add the small pieces of	**chopped hare**
Rolled in	**seasoned flour**
Brown the hare and add and	**1 glass red wine** **1 glass stock**
Season with	**thyme** **salt and pepper**

Cover the pan and cook slowly
for an hour

Shake the sauce and pour into
a bowl and serve with the
noodles.

8 *Agnolotti alla Poggio Gherardo*

Home-made Ravioli with minced chicken (truffle), butter
and cream

Mince finely, twice	1½ lb. cooked chicken
sweat	½ chopped onion
in	4 oz. butter

Stir butter and onion into the
chicken and add

salt and pepper
pinch of tarragon
(1 chopped white truffle
optional)
1 sherry glass of dry white
vermouth
4 fluid oz. cream (single)

Work the mixture to a paste

Make a pound of pasta (see p.
162) divide it and roll it paper
thin. Leave it to rest for half
an hour and then put
teaspoonfuls of the chicken
mixture on one piece of pasta
at about two-inch distances,
brush very lightly in between
with egg-wash and lay the

second sheet of pasta lightly on top. Press down round the little heaps and then cut out with a knife or one of those small scooped wheels.

Have ready a large saucepan of boiling salted water and put in it the ravioli. Boil slowly for about eight minutes, take them out with a strainer, season with melted butter and Parmesan cheese. Serve very hot.

9 Crescioni

Little pasta turnovers filled with spinach, herbs and cream and deep fried

Wash and boil

$1\frac{1}{2}$ lb. spinach

Drain well, pressing the spinach dry with the back of a wooden spoon. Roughly chop the spinach and put it in a frying-pan with

3 tablespoons very good olive oil
2 small cloves garlic, chopped
grated nutmeg
salt and pepper
1 tablespoon fresh chopped herbs such as marjoram, chervil and chives
2 tablespoons grated Parmesan

Mix the spinach and the ingredients, simmer for five minutes, remove from the stove and leave to cool

Meanwhile make pasta as described on p. 162 and roll it out thin as paper, leave it to rest for half an hour and cut into three-inch squares. (Thinly rolled puff pastry will also do quite well.) Put a little heap of spinach on one square at a time and fold over like a turnover, brushing the edges with egg-wash. Seal the edges firmly and, when they are all prepared, deep fry them for three minutes on each side in not too hot oil until lightly coloured. Dust with grated Parmesan and serve on a napkin with a fresh purée of tomatoes (twelve ripe tomatoes squashed into a saucepan, seasoned, covered and stewed for ten minutes, pass through the Mouli).

10 *Tagliatelle alla Romagnola*

Thin strip noodles *fettucini,* with garlic, tomatoes and small garlic sausages

Cook a pound of *fettucini* or homemade pasta, cut into strips, in boiling salted water until just soft (fifteen to twenty minutes). Meanwhile make the following sauce with sausages

In a thick frying-pan heat

3 tablespoons olive oil

In it fry gently

3 cloves garlic, chopped parsley
twelve small fresh garlic sausages or good butcher's sausages

When the sausages are nearly cooked
add

1 tin tomatoes (14–16 oz.)
salt and pepper to taste

Let the sauce and sausages stew for ten minutes

Drain the *fettucini* and lay in a dish making a well in the middle. Arrange the sausages and sauce in the middle and sprinkle with grated Parmesan. Serve very hot.

Soups

❦

Zuppe

Almost all the soups in this book have a basic form of onion and potato, a further vegetable and stock added later. Potato, I find, is a better thickening for soup than flour partly because it is a vegetable itself and not a cereal and also because the consistency is fresher and more palatable. Today the use of electric blenders, which save much time and labour, has revived the serving of delicious home-made soups.

1   Minestra di asparagi

Asparagus Soup

It would be extravagant to use bunches of asparagus just for soup unless you have a garden with weak shoots that are too thin to eat as a vegetable or can buy the sprue asparagus from the shops. Ideal, however, is to use the trimmings from asparagus when they are to be prepared as a vegetable, those white stalky ends

Cut off, then, the thick white stalks of the asparagus (about one third of the length) and wash them. (Boil the green parts as recommended in the asparagus section but reserve a few tips for garnishing the soup.) Alternatively use two pounds of sprue, reserve and boil the very tips and use the rest for the soup

In a thick-based saucepan melt
add
and

and the

2 oz. butter	
1 small onion, chopped	
3 medium potatoes, peeled and sliced	
asparagus trimmings or sprue	

Season lightly with
and cover with a lid

salt and pepper

Sweat for fifteen minutes, remove the lid and add

2 pints milk

Stir and add a small bunch of

parsley

Bring to the boil and simmer for fifteen minutes. Pass through a fine Mouli or seive. Return to a saucepan, bring to

the boil, correct the seasoning
and the consistency with a
little cream and garnish with
tops of asparagus. Serve with
fried croûtons.

2   *Minestra di cavolo e maiale*

Cabbage and pork soup

This, as with many soups is
open to different combinations
but be careful with this soup
(as, indeed, with any other
vegetable soup) that it is not
over-cooked for the flavour
becomes stale.

Remove the stalk from	½ small white cabbage or ¼ large one
Cut the cabbage in two or three slices and shred it finely	
Finely chop	½ lb. piece salt streaky or mild, streaky bacon
Put it in a saucepan with	1 tablespoon dripping or butter
Lightly fry the bacon with add the and	1 shredded onion shredded cabbage freshly milled pepper

Stir the cabbage over the fire for a few minutes and then add

2 pints stock or water

Bring to the boil and simmer for

twenty minutes

Skim from time to time. A few minutes before serving correct the seasoning and add

1 finely sliced cooking apple crushed chestnuts

and/or a few

3 *Minestra di carote*

Carrot Soup

In a thick pan (with a lid) melt add

**2 oz. butter
1 roughly chopped onion
4 large peeled and chopped carrots
1 small peeled and chopped turnip
twelve crushed coriander seeds**

Season lightly with

salt and pepper

Cover with a lid and heat gently for twenty minutes, then add

2 pints stock or water and chicken bouillon

Bring to the boil and simmer for twelve minutes. Pass the soup through a medium mesh Mouli or strainer, return to the saucepan and reboil. Correct the seasoning and consistency with a little more stock and finish with

$\frac{1}{2}$ **cup chopped herbs (a combination of chives, parsley, chervil, marjoram, thyme or rosemary)**

Serve with fried crôutons.

4 *Minestra di cetriolo alla crema*

Cucumber and cream Soup

Peel strips of skin from and liquidise with

**1 cucumber
1 large or 2 small dill pickled cucumbers**

and

**juice of a lemon
$\frac{1}{2}$ onion grated**

After liquidising stir in

**6 fluid oz. cream
salt and pepper
1 tablespoon chopped dill**

If necessary add a squeeze of lemon juice. Keep chilled and serve with a little diced cucumber in the soup.

5 *Minestra di lenti*

Lentil Soup (It is important to have a good chicken or meat stock for this soup)

Soak half a pound of lentils for a few hours in warm water

Into a saucepan, put

**1 onion roughly chopped
1 chopped stick of celery
1 carrot finely chopped
½ lb. brown lentils
(soaked)
4 pints good stock**

Bring to the boil and simmer for an hour to an hour and a half, until the lentils are soft. The stock will have reduced by about a pint. Skim, and season with the following mixture:

In a bowl mix

**6 finely chopped
anchovies
1 chopped clove of garlic
2 tablespoons chopped
parsley
6 leaves sage, chopped
4 fluid oz. good olive oil
twelve roughly crushed
peppercorns**

Stir this mixture well into the soup; remove from the fire and allow to rest (the lentils will absorb some of the oil). Reheat before serving and mix well.

6 *Minestra di lattuga*

Lettuce Soup
(A good summer soup hot or cold, but if served cold reduce
the amount of potato. Use lettuces that remain
underdeveloped in the garden, the leaves of ones that have
just bolted or the outside leaves of about three lettuces)

In a saucepan melt	**2 oz. butter**
add	**1 medium sized onion, chopped**
and	**3 medium peeled and diced potatoes**

Cover with a lid and stew
gently for twenty minutes

Remove the lid and add	**2 pints chicken stock or water and chicken bouillon**

Bring to the boil and add the	**roughly chopped lettuce leaves** **a small bunch of chervil** **pepper and salt (if necessary)**

Boil for ten minutes and then pass through the fine Mouli. Return to the saucepan and before serving add	**6 oz. cream (thin)** **chopped chives and chervil**

7 *Minestra di piselli*

Pea Soup
(An easy soup to make using the pods and the peas but a
good Mouli is essential)

In a saucepan put

**3 lb. peas in their pods
roughly crushed
1 grated onion
small bunch of sweet
herbs**

Add

**3 pints boiling water
salt and pepper**

Bring to the boil and boil
uncovered for half an hour.
Boil fiercely to keep the colour
of the peas. Pass the soup
through a course Mouli and
then through the fine. Return
to the saucepan and reboil for
five minutes

Correct the seasoning, add
and serve with fried bread
croûtons.

3 tablespoons thick cream

8 *Minestra di zucca*

Pumpkin Soup
(A spiced soup)

Peel and roughly dice a	**2 lb. slice of yellow pumpkin**
Put it in a saucepan with and	**2 oz. butter** **1 chopped onion** **twelve coriander seeds** **large pinch cumin** **salt and ground pepper** **1 medium potato peeled and chopped**
Cover with a lid and simmer for twenty minutes. Remove the lid, add	**3 pints stock or water and chicken bouillon**

Bring to the boil and simmer for thirty minutes, uncovered. Pass the soup through the coarse disc of the Mouli, return to the pan and reboil. Check the seasoning and add fresh milled pepper a small spoonful of cream for each bowl and chopped parsley.

9   *Cream of Onion Soup*

Melt, in a saucepan   **2 oz. butter**

Peel and chop   **5 medium-sized onions**

Put the onions in the saucepan with

3 peeled and diced potatoes (medium sized) salt, pepper and nutmeg

Cover with a lid and stew gently for
add
and bring to the boil

**twenty minutes
2 pints chicken stock**

Boil for ten minutes and pass through a fine Mouli. Return to the saucepan and add

½ pint single cream

Correct the seasoning and garnish with chopped parsley and fried bread croûtons.

10   *Minestra di carciofi di Giudea*

Jerusalem Artichoke Soup

Peel and slice into a bowl of cold water (with a piece of lemon)

6 good-sized Jerusalem artichokes

Peel and chop	**1 onion**
Melt, in a saucepan	**2 oz. butter**
Add the onion and Jerusalem artichoke and season lightly with	**salt and pepper**
Cover with a lid and simmer gently for ten minutes	
Remove the lid and add	**2 pints of milk**
Bring to the boil. Simmer gently for a further ten minutes and pass the soup through the fine Mouli. Return the soup to the saucepan. Reboil and correct the seasoning, add a little	**single cream chopped chervil**

and fried bread croûtons, before serving.

11 *Polentina alla Veneziana*

Maize-flour Soup

Bring to the boil and skim	**3 pints good chicken broth**
Mix into a little of the stock	**3 tablespoons polenta (fine maize flour)**

Stir to a paste

Stir the paste carefully into the
stock then gradually add   **3 oz. butter**

Serve with fried bread
croûtons.

12 *Minestra di acetosa*

Sorrel Soup

In a saucepan melt   **2 oz. butter**
add   **2 peeled and chopped
                                  onions**
and   **3 peeled and chopped
                                  potatoes**

Season with   **salt and pepper**

Cover with a lid, simmer gently
for twenty minutes. Remove
the lid and add   **3 pints chicken stock
                                  ½ lb. washed sorrel**

Bring to the boil and simmer
for five minutes. Pass through
a coarse Mouli and serve with
croûtons and a little cream
added to each bowl of soup.

13 *Minestra di crescione*

Watercress Soup

In a saucepan melt	**2 oz. butter**
add	**1 onion peeled and chopped**
	3 medium sized potatoes
and the stalks of	**3 bunches watercress**

Cover with a lid and season
with **salt and pepper**
and stew gently for twenty
minutes.
Remove the lid and add **2 pints chicken stock**
and the remainder of the
watercress. Bring to the boil
and cook for ten minutes, pass
through the medium Mouli and
return to the saucepan and add **½ pint single cream**
Correct the seasoning and
consistency. Garnish with
chopped parsley.

14 *Minestra di spinaci*

Spinach Soup

Into	**3 pints chicken stock**
put	**2 medium sized potatoes (peeled and sliced)**

and

1 bunch chopped spring onions

Bring to the boil and cook for twenty minutes and add

1 lb. spinach, washed and roughly chopped

and a little grated nutmeg. Cook for a further ten minutes. Pass through a coarse Mouli and season. Finish with a little cream cheese softened with cream.

15 *Minestra di pomodori*

Tomato Soup

In a saucepan melt add

2 oz. butter
1 onion peeled and chopped

and

1 medium-sized potato, peeled and chopped

Cover with a lid and simmer gently for twenty minutes

Remove the lid and add and

3 lb. ripe tomatoes
1 pint chicken stock
(or to make a quick soup—1 large tin Italian peeled tomatoes)

Bring to the boil and simmer for ten minutes, pass through a medium mouli and return to

the saucepan. Re-season
adding a pinch of sugar and
garnish with a little chopped
basil, marjoram or parsley.

16 *Minestra di verdura, erbe e crema*

Vegetable, herb and cream Soup

Into a saucepan melt add	**2 oz. butter** **2 chopped sticks celery** **1 chopped leek** **1 chopped carrot**
Season with salt and pepper, cover with a lid and stew gently for twenty minutes. Add	**3 pints chicken stock** **1 roughly chopped lettuce** **$\frac{1}{4}$ lb. sorrel or spinach, washed and chopped**
Bring to the boil and simmer for ten minutes. Pass through the medium Mouli and return to the saucepan. Reboil, correct the seasoning and add	**3 tablespoons chopped herbs** **(which might include, chervil, chives, marjoram and a little thyme or tarragon)**
Add a little cream before serving.	

Index

About the Authors

Michael Waterfield is a cook of renown and a restaurateur. He is the owner of the Wife of Bath Restaurant at Wye, in Kent, England, where almost all of the dishes in this book have been served.

Janet Ross was born in 1842 and died in 1927. She married Henry Ross and they lived in Tuscany in a villa outside of Florence.

FEAST TO YOUR HEART'S DELIGHT!

BALLANTINE'S COOKIN' GOOD!